HAL•LEONARD GUITAR PLAY-ALONG

VOL. 111

JOHN MELLENCAMP

Tracking, mixing, and mastering by
Jake Johnson & Bill Maynard at Paradyme Productions
All Guitars by Doug Boduch
Bass by Tom McGirr
Keyboards by Warren Wiegratz
Drums by Scott Schroedl

Cover photo: Robb D. Cohen/Retna, LTD

ISBN 978-1-4234-6873-8

HAL•LEONARD® CORPORATION

7777 W. BLUEMOUND RD. P.O. BOX 13819 MILWAUKEE, WI 53213

In Australia Contact:
Hal Leonard Australia Pty. Ltd.
4 Lentara Court
Cheltenham, Victoria, 3192 Australia
Email: ausadmin@halleonard.com.au

Visit Hal Leonard Online at
www.halleonard.com

VOL. 111

CONTENTS

Guitar Notation Legend

THE MUSICAL STAFF shows pitches and rhythms and is divided by bar lines into measures. Pitches are named after the first seven letters of the alphabet.

TABLATURE graphically represents the guitar fingerboard. Each horizontal line represents a string, and each number represents a fret.

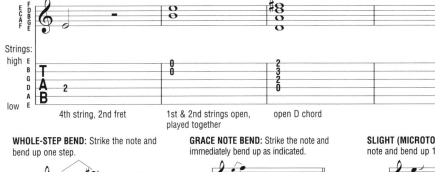

4th string, 2nd fret   1st & 2nd strings open, played together   open D chord

HALF-STEP BEND: Strike the note and bend up 1/2 step.

WHOLE-STEP BEND: Strike the note and bend up one step.

GRACE NOTE BEND: Strike the note and immediately bend up as indicated.

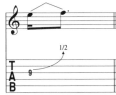

SLIGHT (MICROTONE) BEND: Strike the note and bend up 1/4 step.

BEND AND RELEASE: Strike the note and bend up as indicated, then release back to the original note. Only the first note is struck.

PRE-BEND: Bend the note as indicated, then strike it.

VIBRATO: The string is vibrated by rapidly bending and releasing the note with the fretting hand.

PALM MUTING: The note is partially muted by the pick hand lightly touching the string(s) just before the bridge.

HAMMER-ON: Strike the first (lower) note with one finger, then sound the higher note (on the same string) with another finger by fretting it without picking.

PULL-OFF: Place both fingers on the notes to be sounded. Strike the first note and without picking, pull the finger off to sound the second (lower) note.

LEGATO SLIDE: Strike the first note and then slide the same fret-hand finger up or down to the second note. The second note is not struck.

SHIFT SLIDE: Same as legato slide, except the second note is struck.

TRILL: Very rapidly alternate between the notes indicated by continuously hammering on and pulling off.

TAPPING: Hammer ("tap") the fret indicated with the pick-hand index or middle finger and pull off to the note fretted by the fret hand.

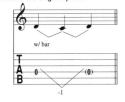

NATURAL HARMONIC: Strike the note while the fret-hand lightly touches the string directly over the fret indicated.

PINCH HARMONIC: The note is fretted normally and a harmonic is produced by adding the edge of the thumb or the tip of the index finger of the pick hand to the normal pick attack.

TREMOLO PICKING: The note is picked as rapidly and continuously as possible.

VIBRATO BAR DIVE AND RETURN: The pitch of the note or chord is dropped a specified number of steps (in rhythm), then returned to the original pitch.

VIBRATO BAR SCOOP: Depress the bar just before striking the note, then quickly release the bar.

VIBRATO BAR DIP: Strike the note and then immediately drop a specified number of steps, then release back to the original pitch.

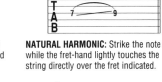

Additional Musical Definitions

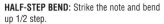 (accent)   • Accentuate note (play it louder).

(staccato)   • Play the note short.

D.S. al Coda   • Go back to the sign (𝄋), then play until the measure marked "*To Coda*," then skip to the section labelled "**Coda**."

D.C. al Fine   • Go back to the beginning of the song and play until the measure marked "*Fine*" (end).

Fill   • Label used to identify a brief melodic figure which is to be inserted into the arrangement.

N.C.   • Harmony is implied.

• Repeat measures between signs.

• When a repeated section has different endings, play the first ending only the first time and the second ending only the second time.

Authority Song

Words and Music by
John Mellencamp

Double drop D tuning:
(low to high) D-A-D-G-B-D

Intro
Moderately fast Rock ♩ = 157

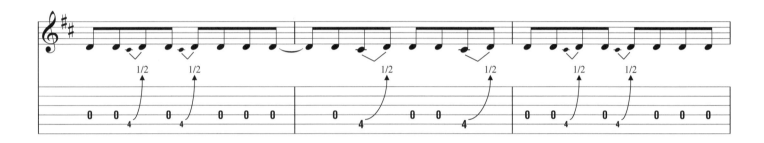

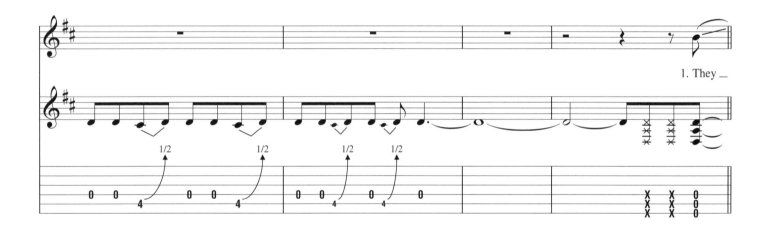

1. They —

Verse

_____ like to get you in a com - pro - mis - ing po - si - tion.

2. *See additional lyrics*

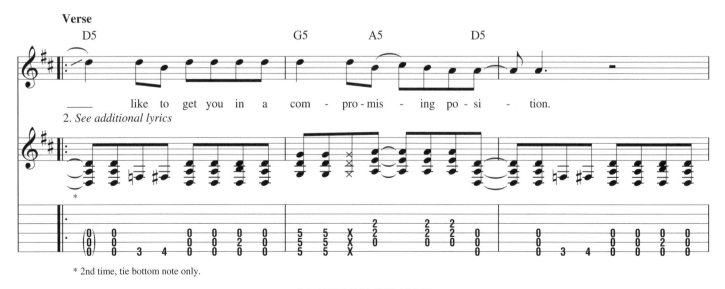

* 2nd time, tie bottom note only.

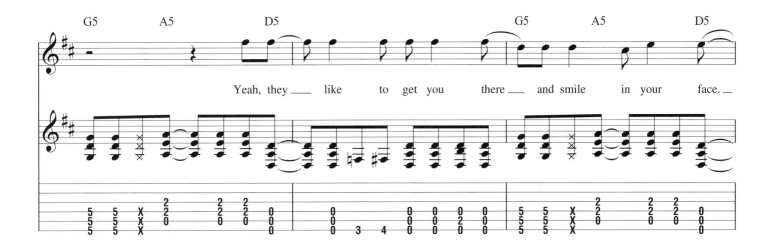

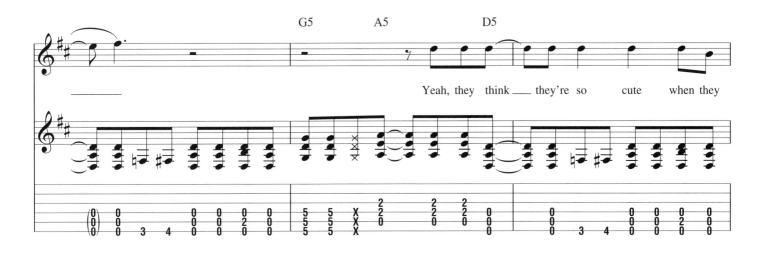

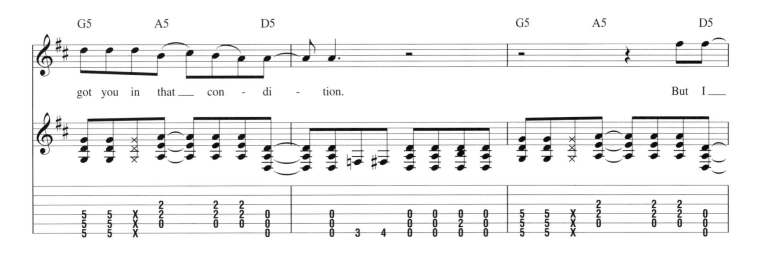

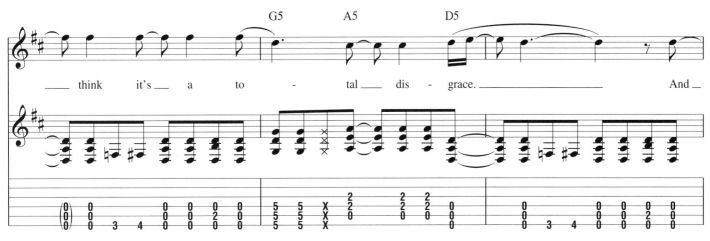

Chorus

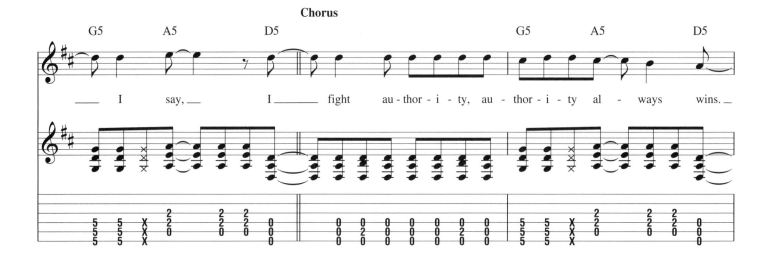

I say, ___ I ___ fight au-thor-i-ty, au-thor-i-ty al-ways wins. ___

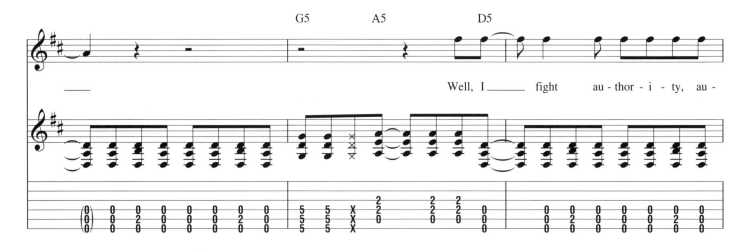

___ Well, I ___ fight au-thor-i-ty, au-

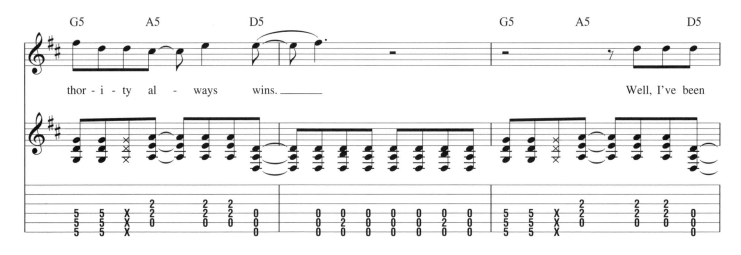

thor-i-ty al-ways wins. ___ Well, I've been

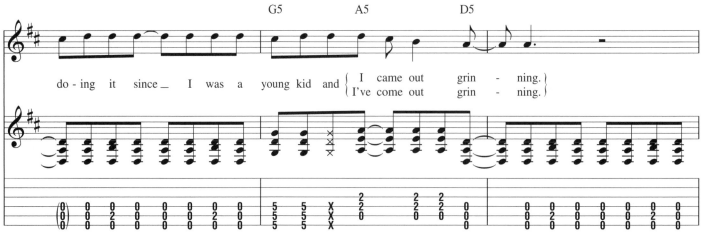

do-ing it since ___ I was a young kid and { I came out grin - ning. / I've come out grin - ning. }

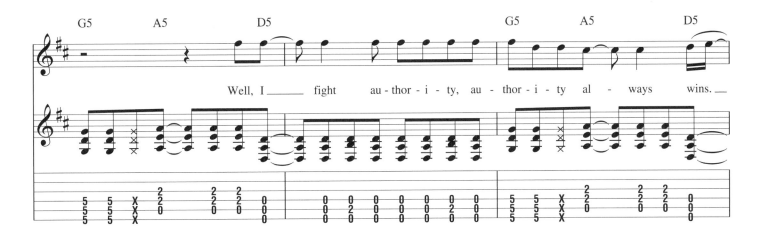

Well, I _____ fight au - thor - i - ty, au - thor - i - ty al - ways wins. _____

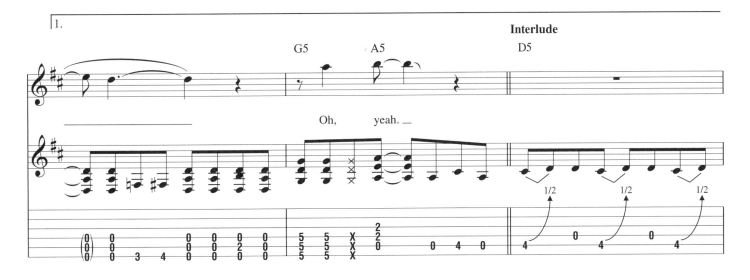

1.

Interlude

Oh, _____ yeah. _____

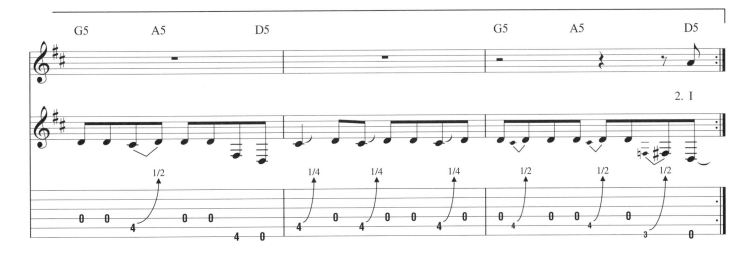

2. I

2.

Guitar Solo

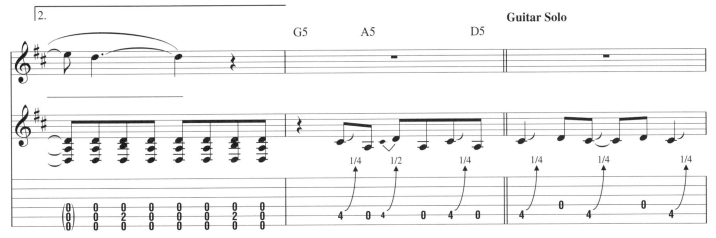

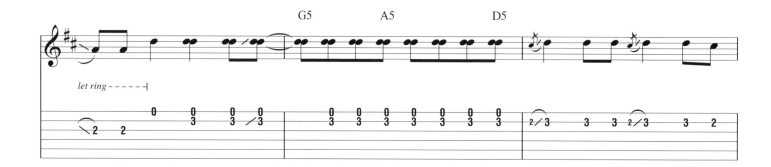

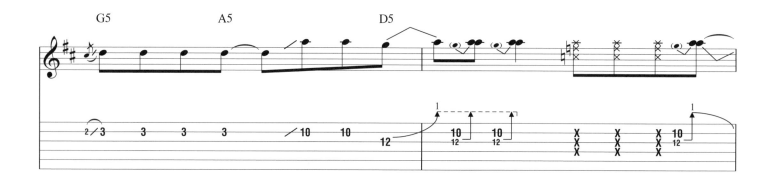

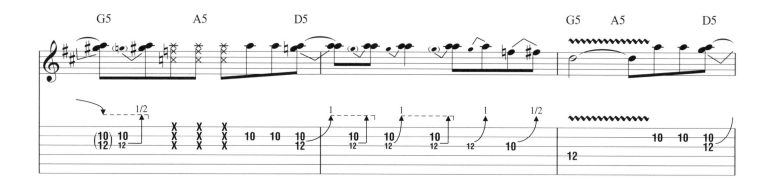

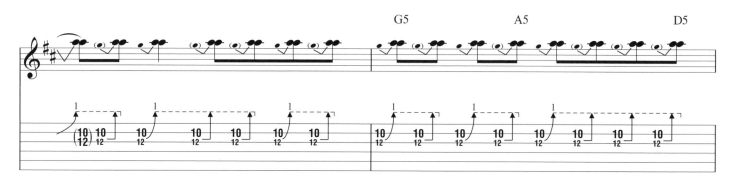

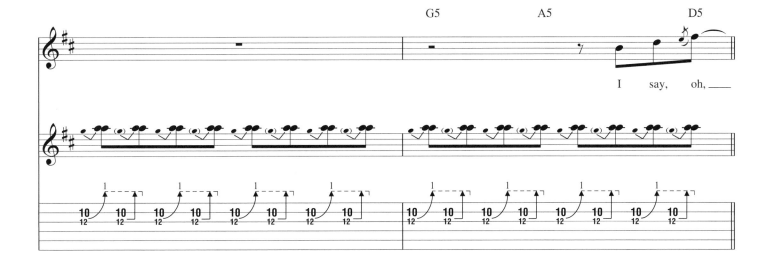

G5   A5   D5

I say, oh, ___

Interlude

N.C.

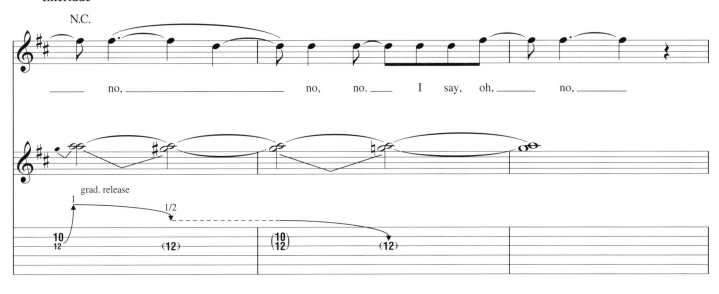

___ no, ___ no, no. ___ I say, oh, ___ no, ___

no, no. ___ I say, oh, ___ no, ___ no, ___ no, no. ___ I

Outro-Chorus

N.C.

fight au - thor - i - ty, au - thor - i - ty al - ways wins. ___ I

___ fight au - thor - i - ty, au - thor - i - ty al - ways wins. ___ Kick it in.

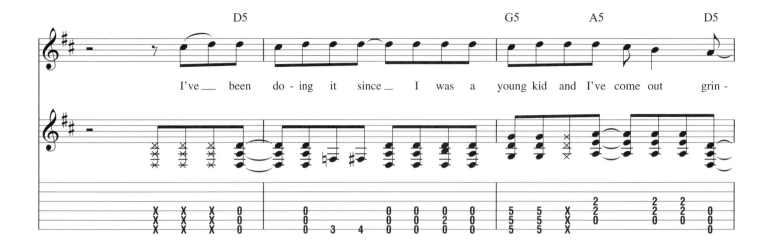

I've ___ been do-ing it since ___ I was a young kid and I've come out grin-

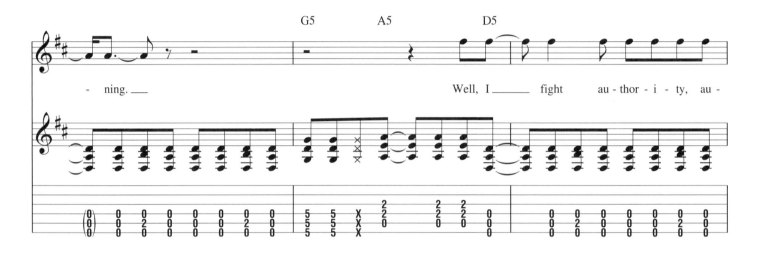

- ning. ___ Well, I ___ fight au-thor-i-ty, au-

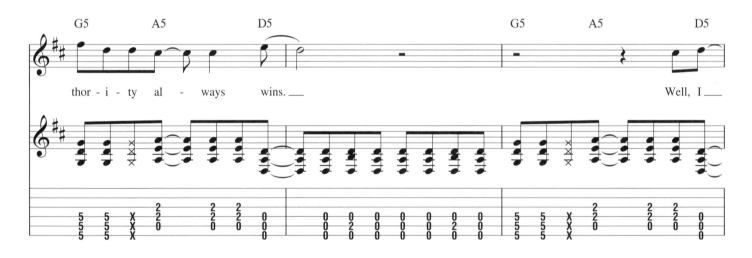

thor-i-ty al - ways wins. ___ Well, I ___

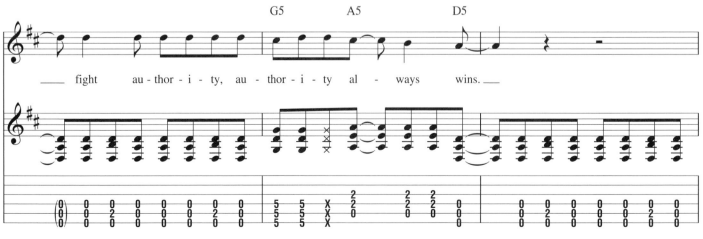

___ fight au-thor-i-ty, au-thor-i-ty al - ways wins. ___

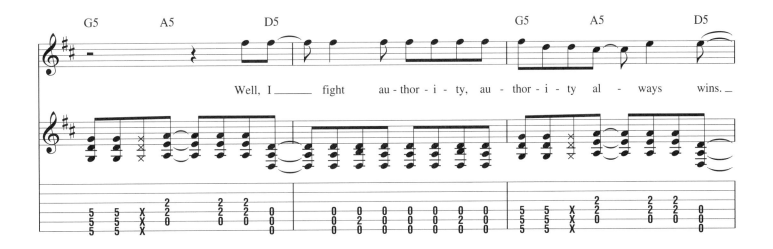

Well, I _____ fight au - thor - i - ty, au - thor - i - ty al - ways wins. _

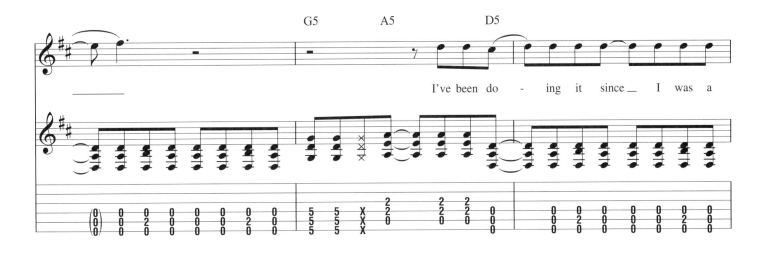

_____ I've been do - ing it since _ I was a

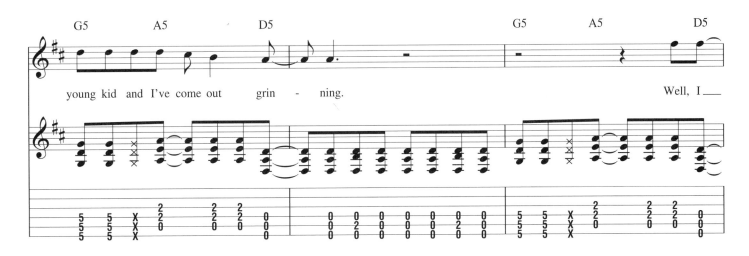

young kid and I've come out grin - ning. Well, I _____

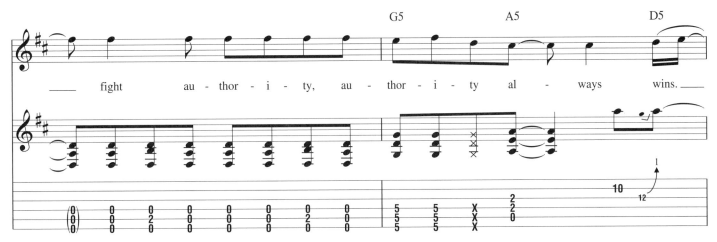

_____ fight au - thor - i - ty, au - thor - i - ty al - ways wins. _

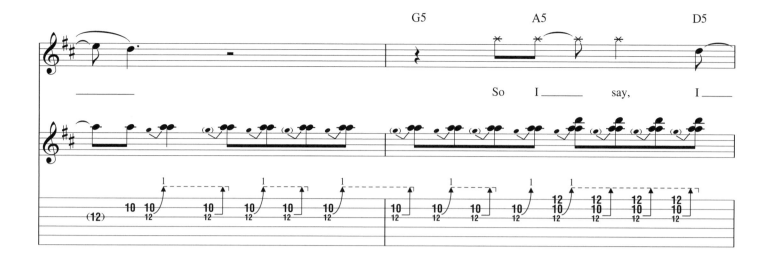

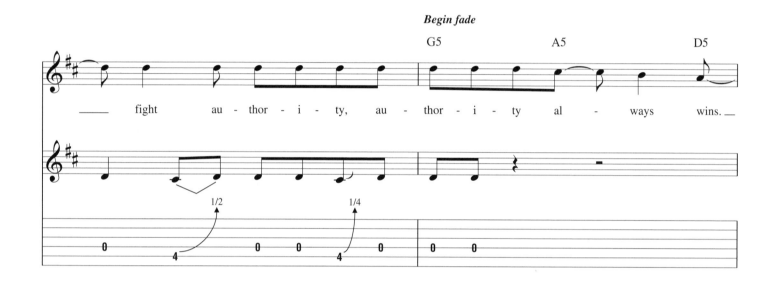

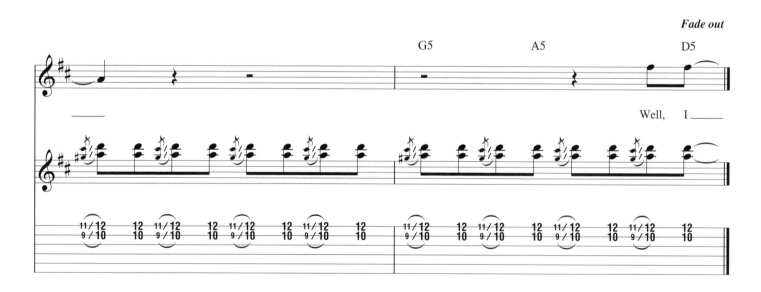

Additional Lyrics

2. I call up my preacher, I say, "Give me strength for round five."
   He said, "You don't need no strength, you need to grow up, son."
   I said, "Growing up leads to growing old and then to dying.
   Ooh, and dying to me don't sound like all that much fun."
   And so I say,...

Hurts So Good

Words and Music by John Mellencamp and George Green

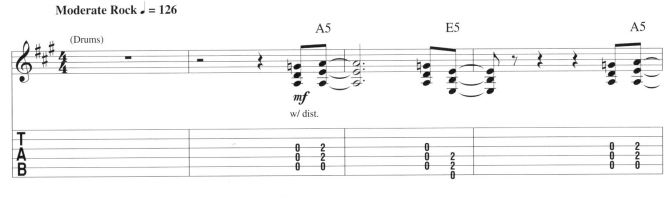

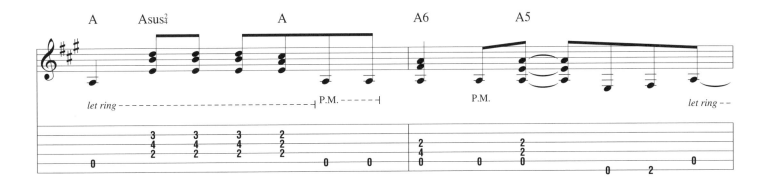

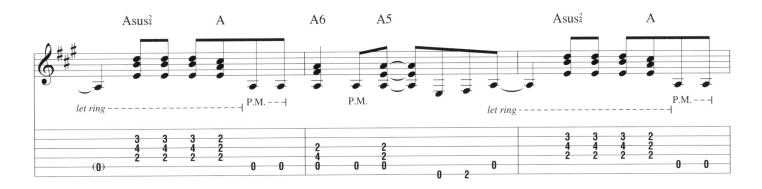

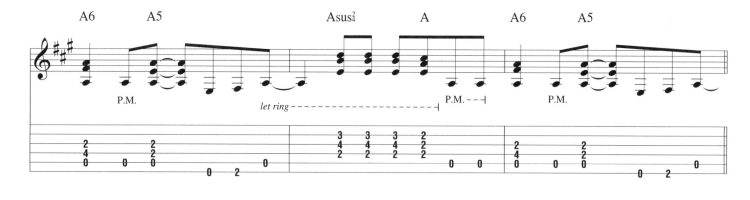

§ Verse

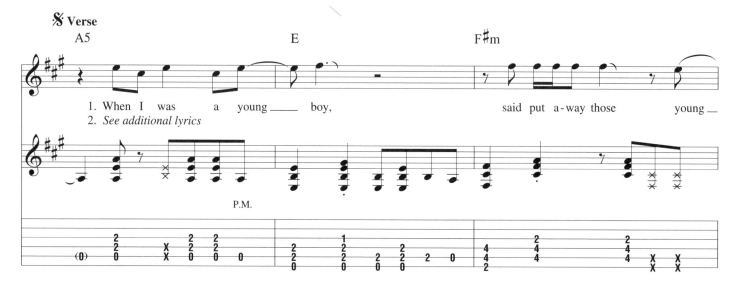

1. When I was a young ____ boy, said put a-way those young ____
2. *See additional lyrics*

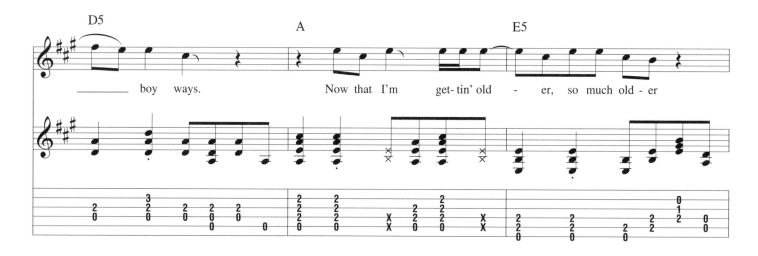

____ boy ways. Now that I'm get-tin' old - er, so much old - er

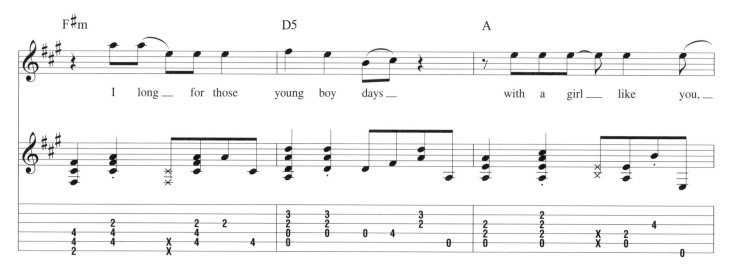

I long ____ for those young boy days ____ with a girl ____ like you, ____

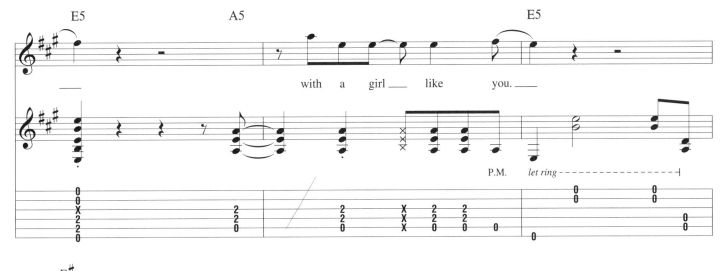

with a girl ___ like ___ you. ___

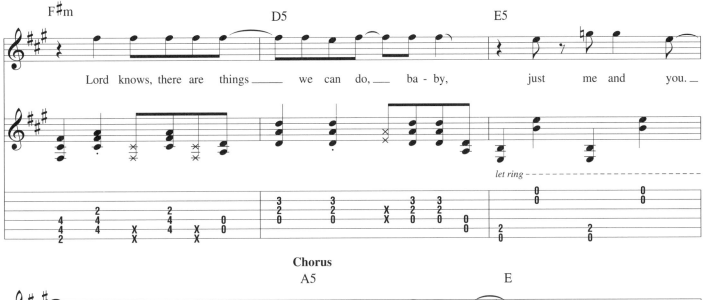

Lord knows, there are things ___ we can do, ___ ba - by, just me and you. ___

Chorus

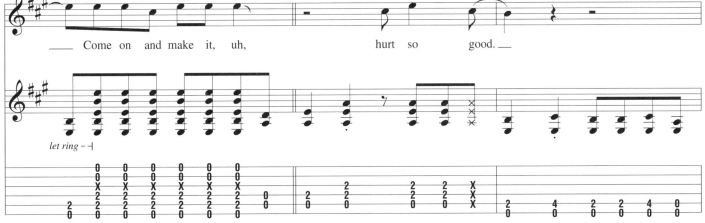

___ Come on and make it, uh, hurt so good. ___

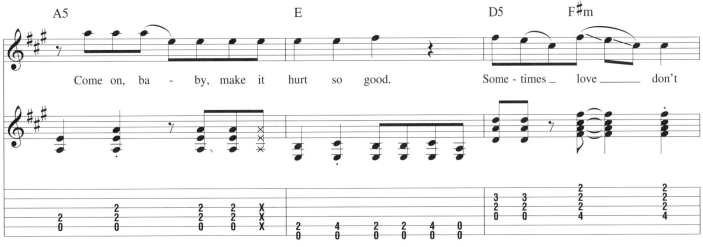

Come on, ba - by, make it hurt so good. Some - times ___ love ___ don't

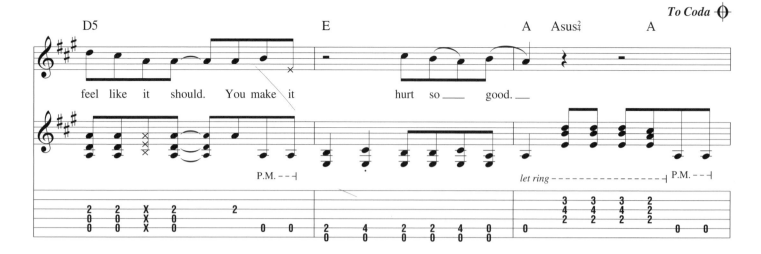

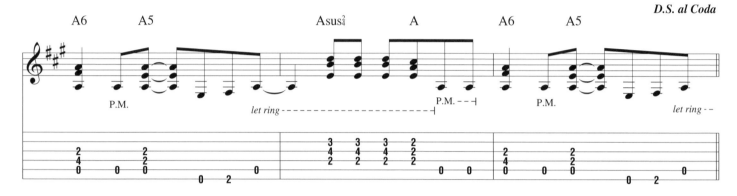

⊕ **Coda**

Bridge

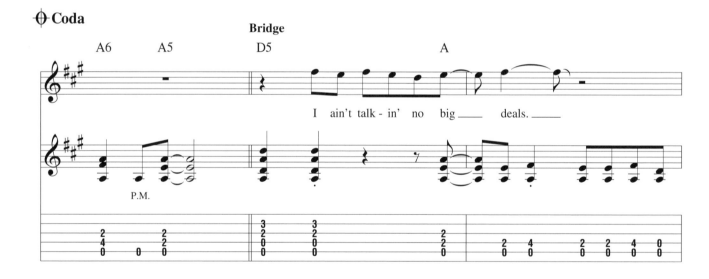

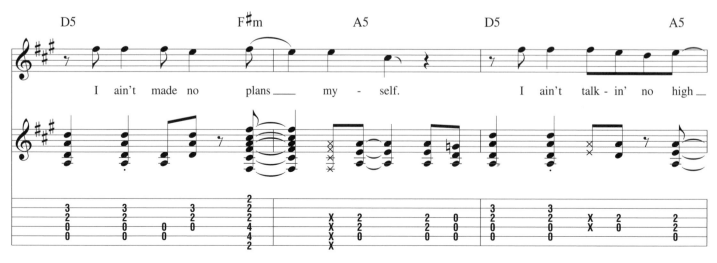

E

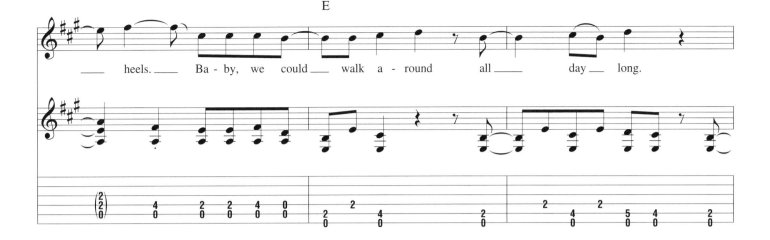

heels. ___ Ba - by, we could ___ walk a - round all ___ day ___ long.

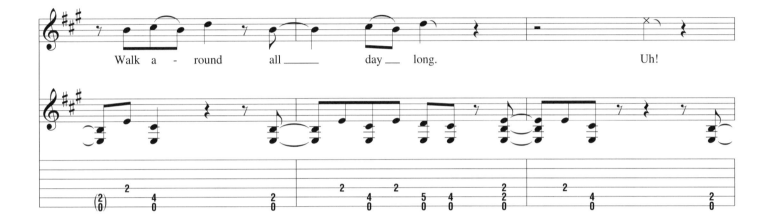

Walk a - round all ___ day ___ long. Uh!

Chorus
A5

Hurts so good. ___

P.M. P.M. ----

19

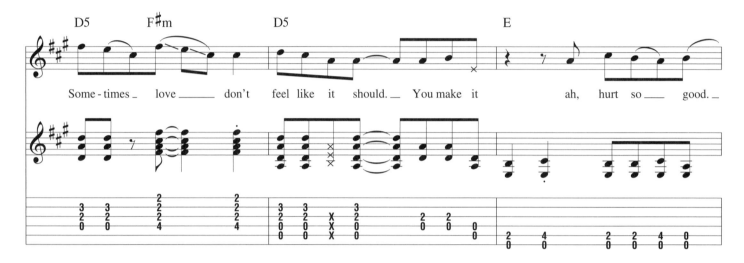

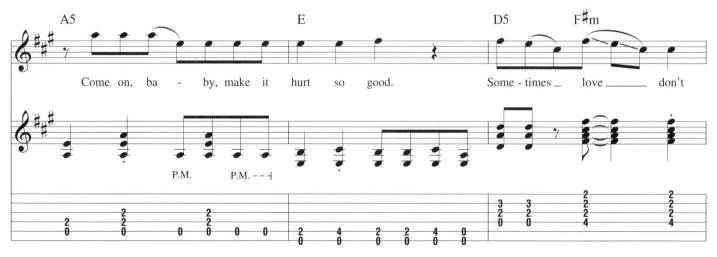

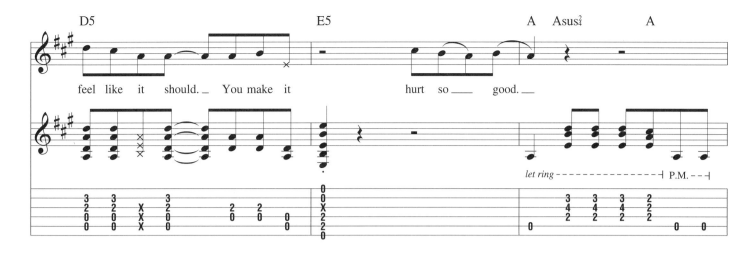

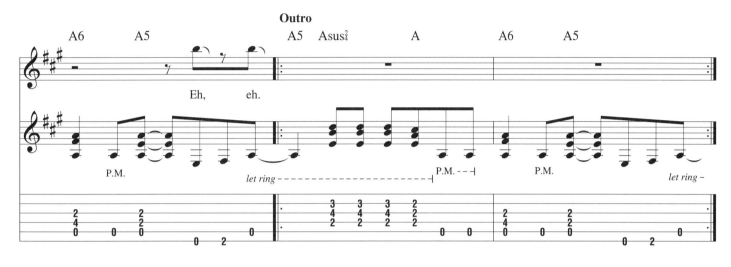

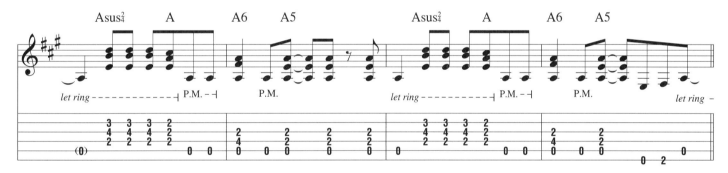

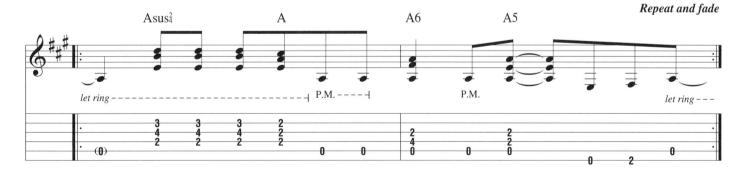

Additional Lyrics

2. Don't have to be so excited,
   Just tryin' to give myself a little bit of fun, yeah.
   You always look so inviting,
   You ain't as green as you are young.
   Hey baby, it's you.
   Come on, girl, now it's you.
   Sink your teeth right through my bones, baby,
   Let's see what we can do.
   Come on and make it, uh.

I Need a Lover

**Words and Music by
John Mellencamp**

Intro

Moderately fast ♩ = 152

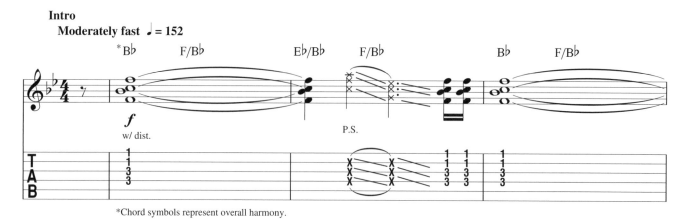

*Chord symbols represent overall harmony.

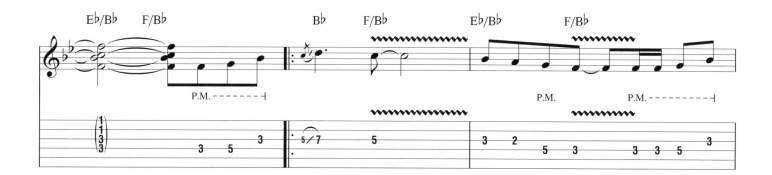

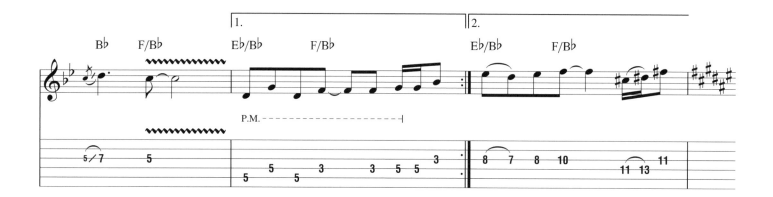

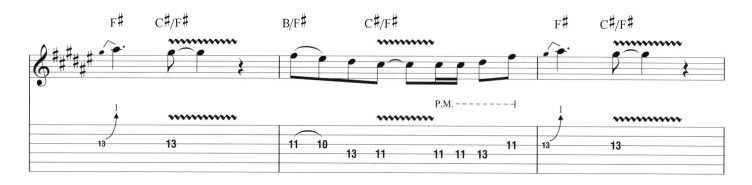

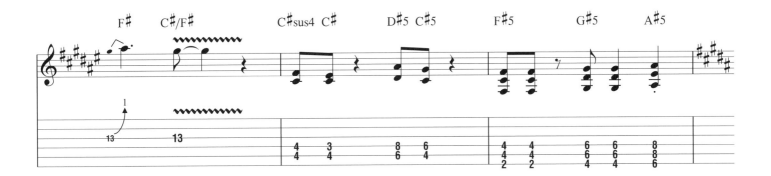

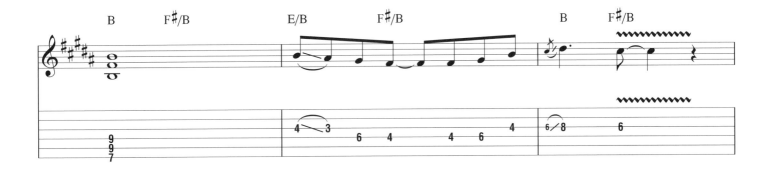

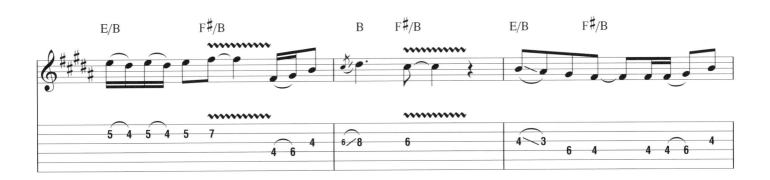

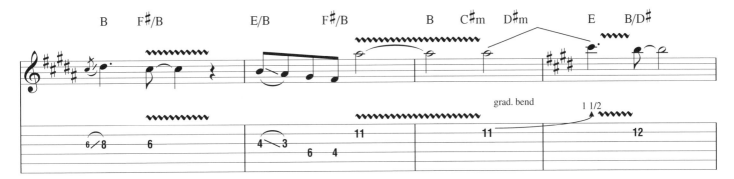

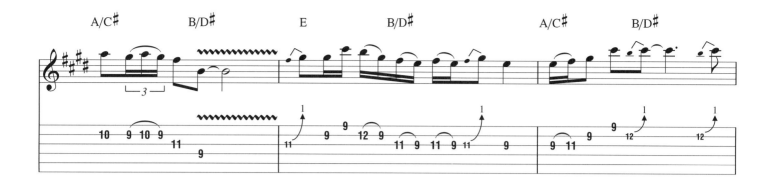

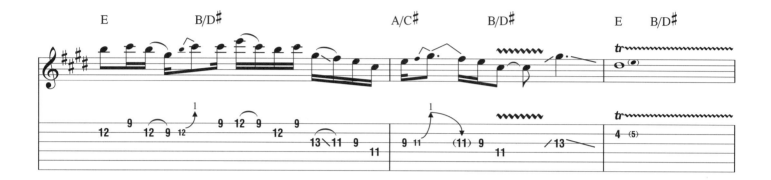

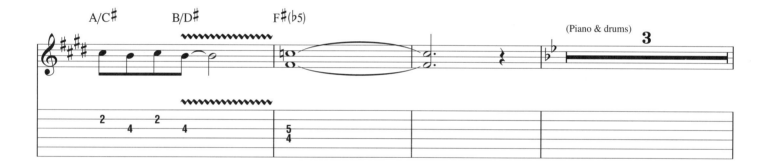

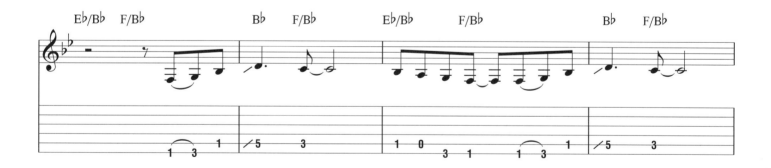

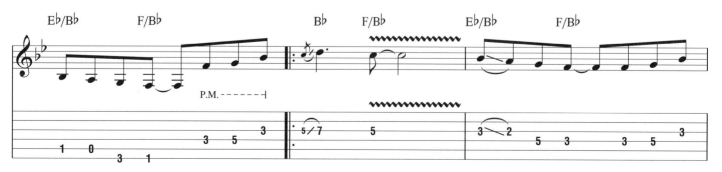

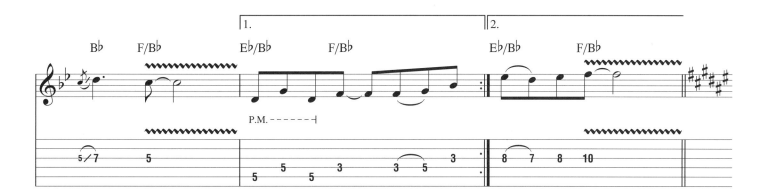

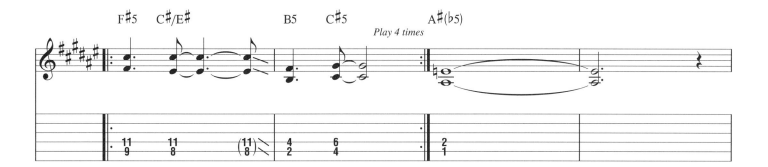

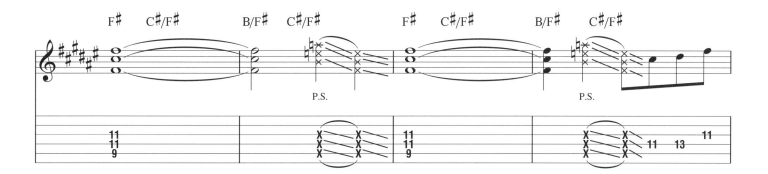

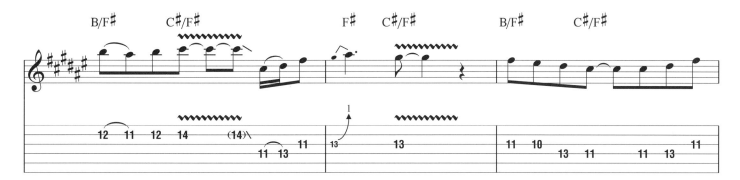

Chorus

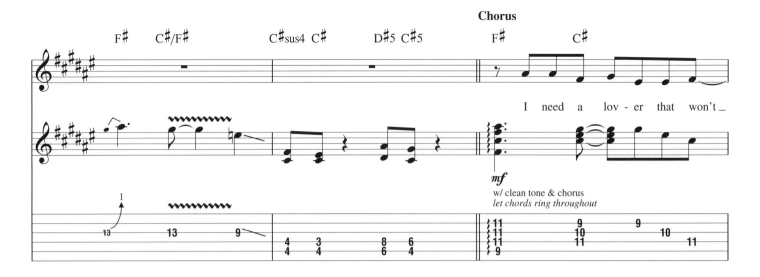

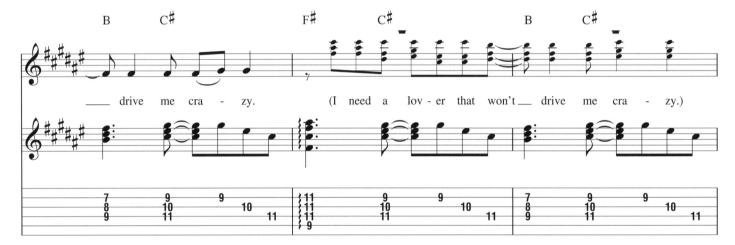

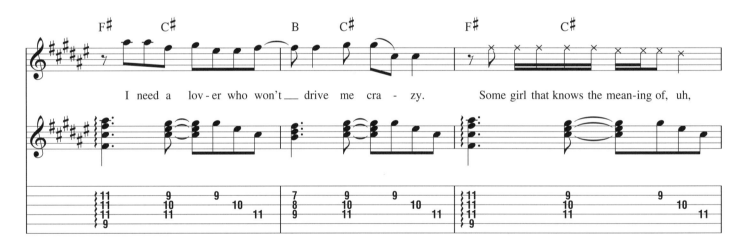

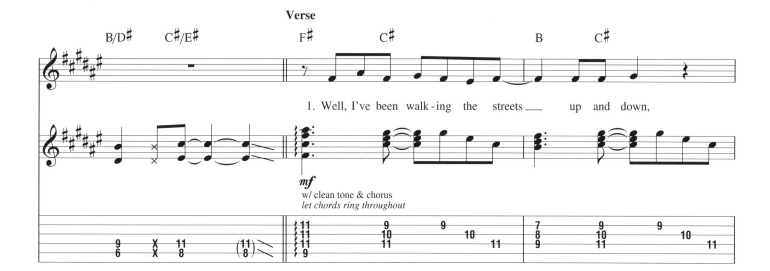

Verse

1. Well, I've been walk-ing the streets __ up and down,

rac-ing through __ the hu-man jun - gle at night. ___ I'm so con - fused, __ my

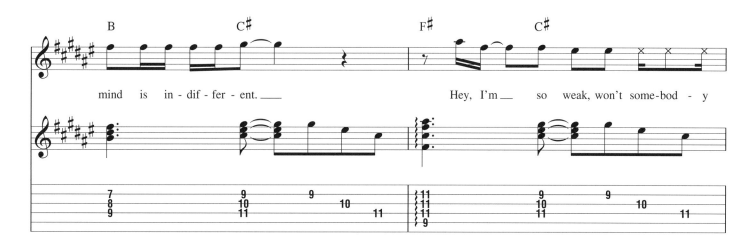

mind is in - dif - fer - ent. ___ Hey, I'm __ so weak, won't some-bod - y

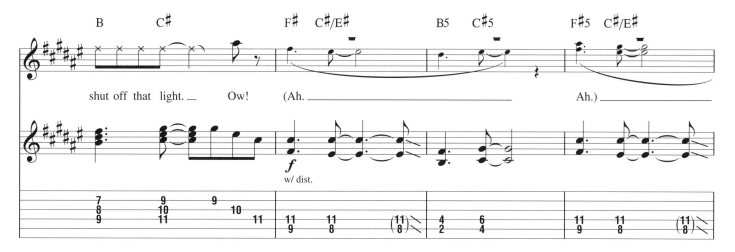

shut off that light. __ Ow! (Ah. _____ Ah.) __

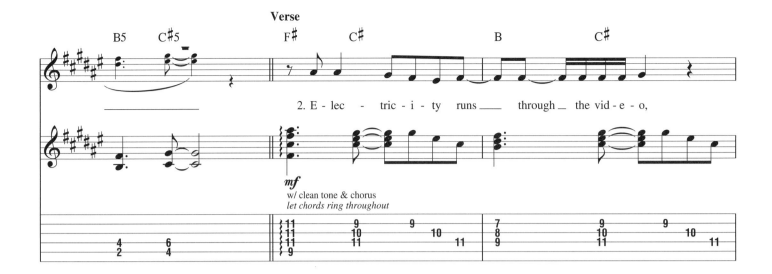

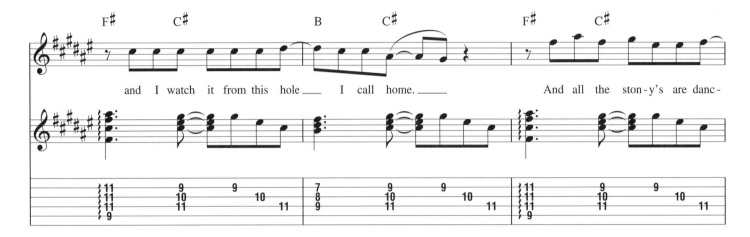

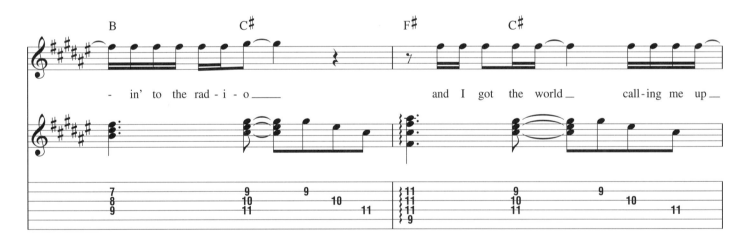

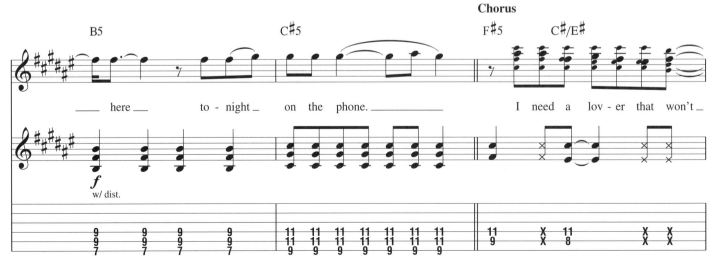

drive me cra - zy. Some girl to thrill me, and then go a - way.

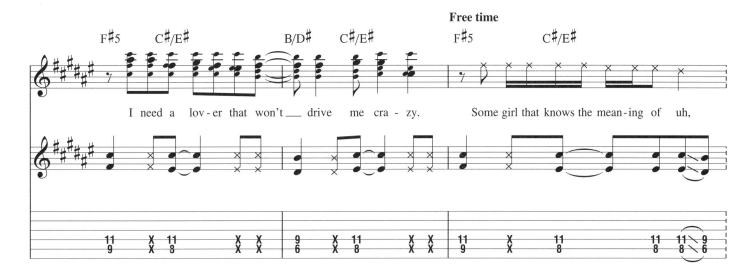

Free time

I need a lov - er that won't __ drive me cra - zy. Some girl that knows the mean - ing of uh,

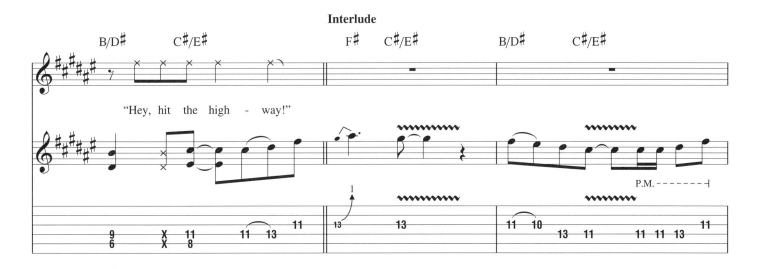

Interlude

"Hey, hit the high - way!"

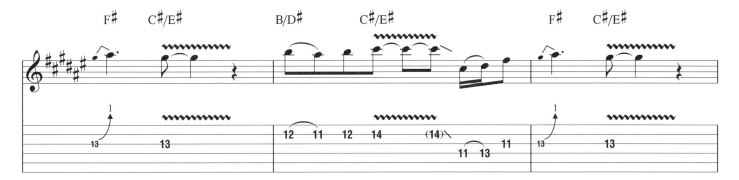

Verse

3. Well, I'm ___ not wiped out by this pool-room life ___ I'm liv-ing.

I'm gon-na quit this job, go to school ___ or head back home. ___

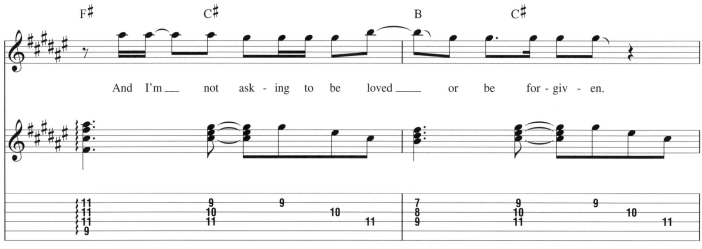

And I'm ___ not ask-ing to be loved ___ or be for-giv-en.

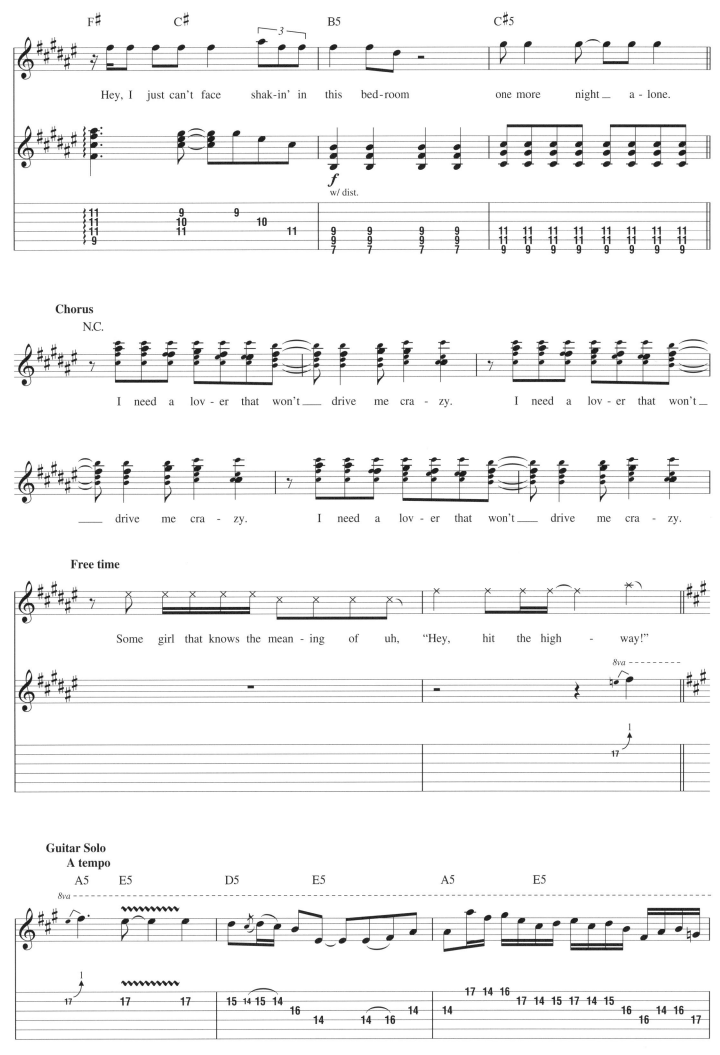

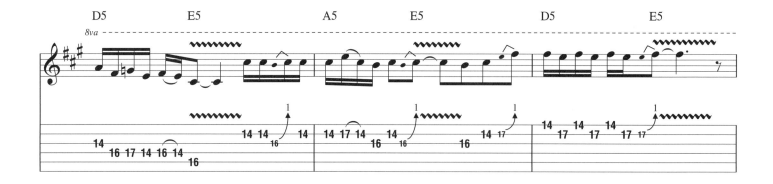

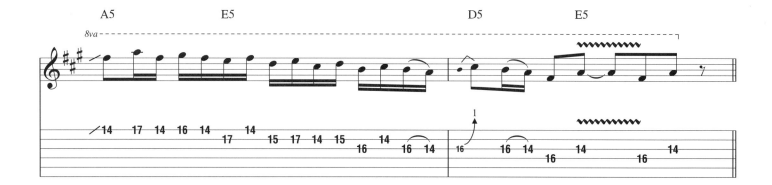

Chorus

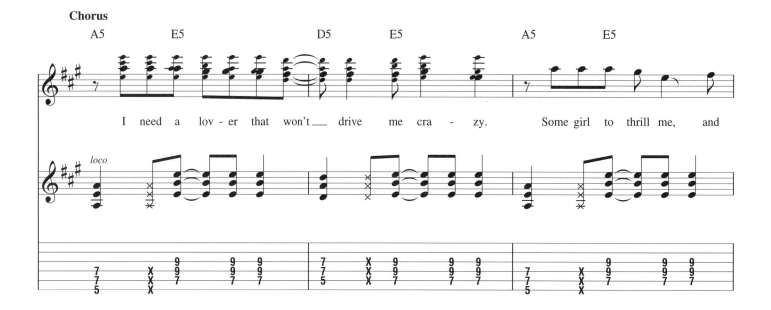

I need a lov-er that won't ___ drive me cra-zy. Some girl to thrill me, and

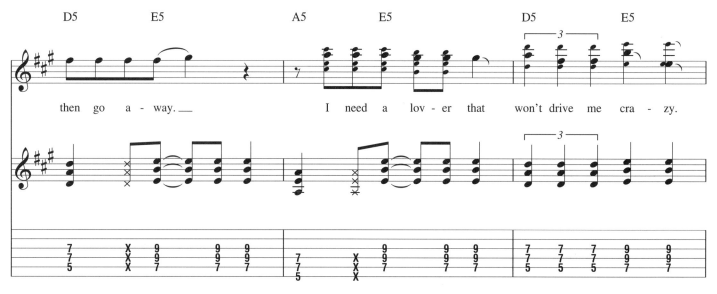

then go a-way. ___ I need a lov-er that won't drive me cra-zy.

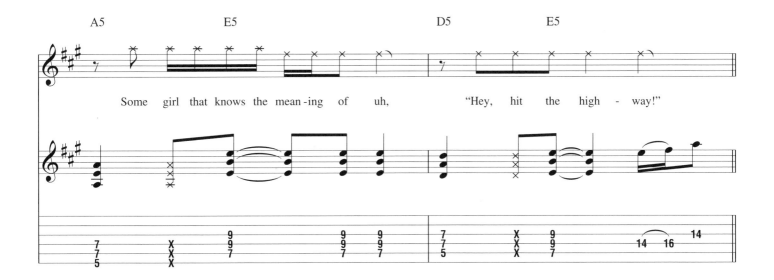

Some girl that knows the mean-ing of uh, "Hey, hit the high - way!"

Outro-Guitar Solo

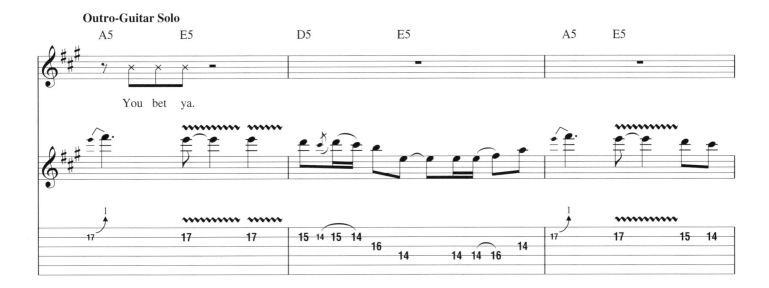

You bet ya.

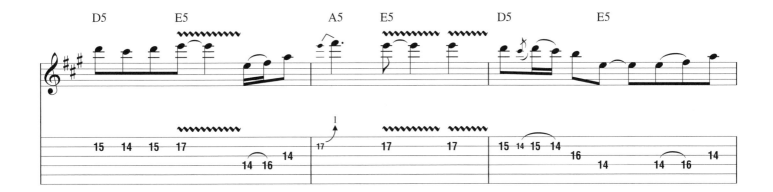

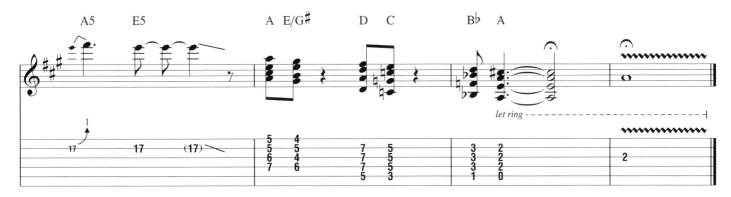

let ring

Jack and Diane

Words and Music by John Mellencamp

2nd time, substitute Fill 1

A Aadd9   E   D   E

Jack - ie say, "Hey Di - ane, let's run off be - hind the shad - y trees. _____

A Aadd9   E   D   E   A

Drib - ble off those Bob - by Brooks, let me do what I please." _ Say, uh,

Chorus

A Aadd9   E   D   E

1. "Oh yeah, ___   life goes ___ on ___
2. *See additional lyrics*

A Aadd9   E   D   E   Esus4 E

long af - ter the thrill of liv - in' is ___ gone." _ They say, uh,

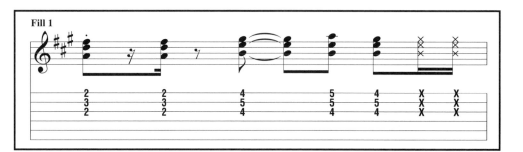

Fill 1

36

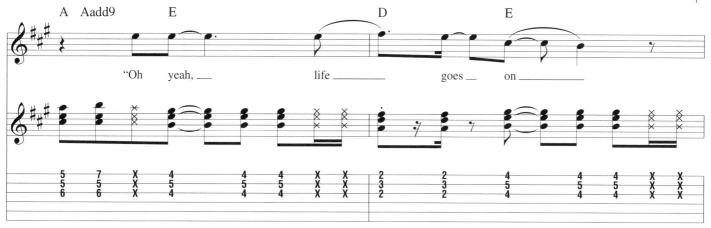

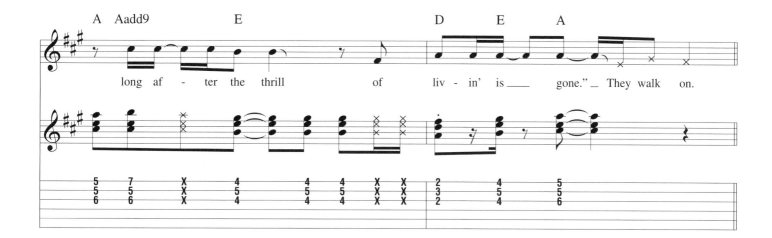

2nd time, D.S. al Coda

Interlude

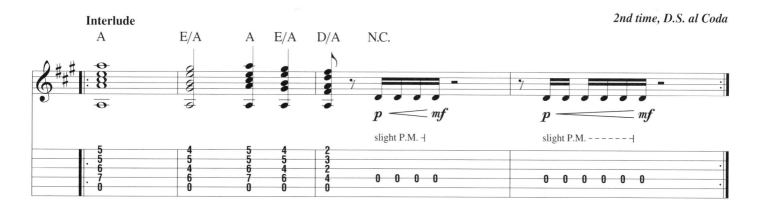

⊕ **Coda**

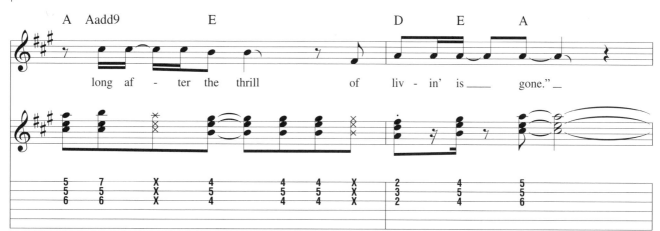

Bridge

So let it rock, let it roll. _____ Let the Bi-ble Belt come and save my soul. _____ Hold on to six-teen as long as you can. _____ Chang-es come a-round real soon, make us wom-en and men. _____

* Vol. swell

Interlude

Chorus

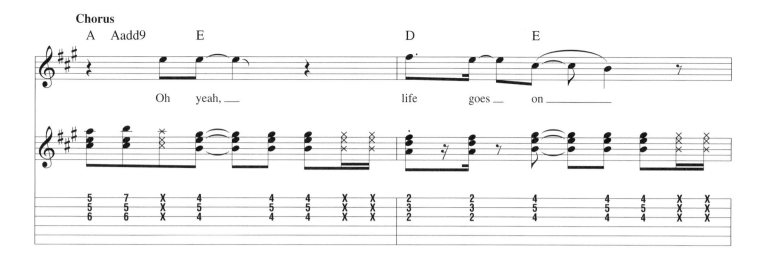

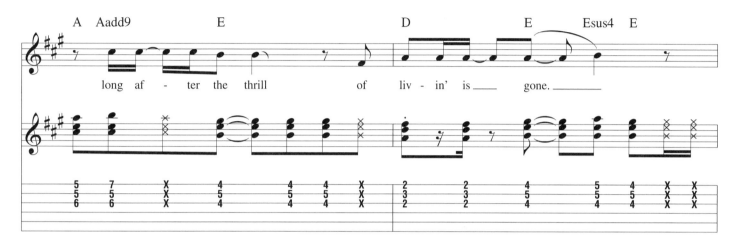

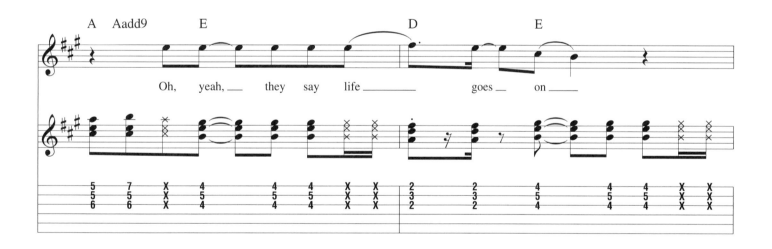

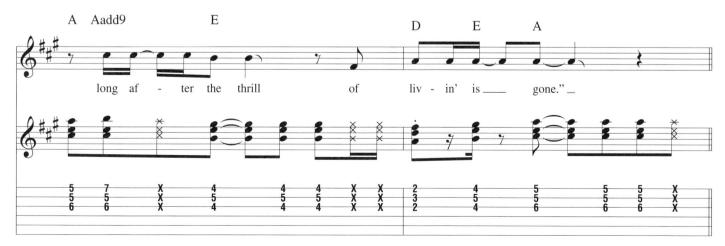

Outro-Verse

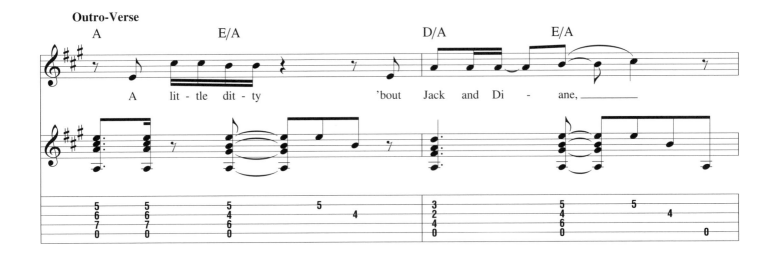

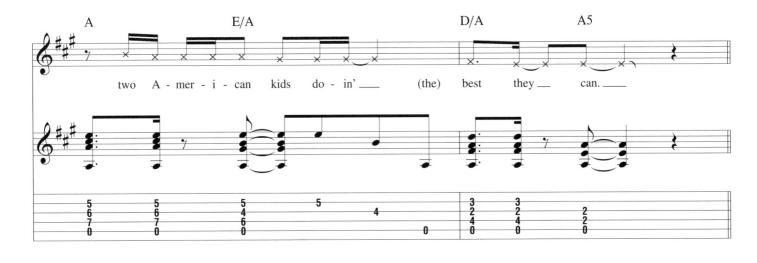

Play 4 times & fade

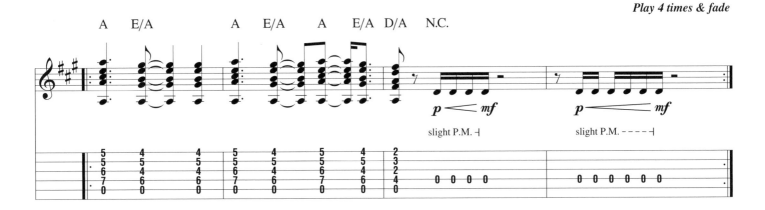

Additional Lyrics

3. Jackie sits back, collects his thoughts for the moment.
   Scratches his head and does his best James Dean.
   "Well, then there Diane, we oughta run off to the city."
   Diane says, "Baby, you ain't missin' nothing." But Jackie say, ah,

Chorus 2. "Oh yeah, life goes on
   Long after the thrill of livin' is gone."
   "Oh yeah," they say, "life goes on
   Long after the thrill of livin' is gone."

Lonely Ol' Night

**Words and Music by
John Mellencamp**

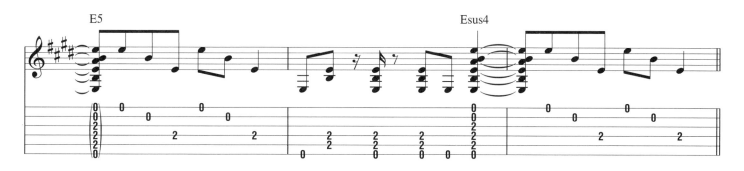

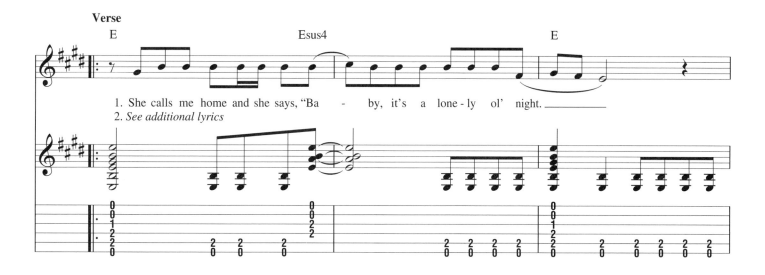

1. She calls me home and she says, "Ba - by, it's a lone - ly ol' night. _____
2. *See additional lyrics*

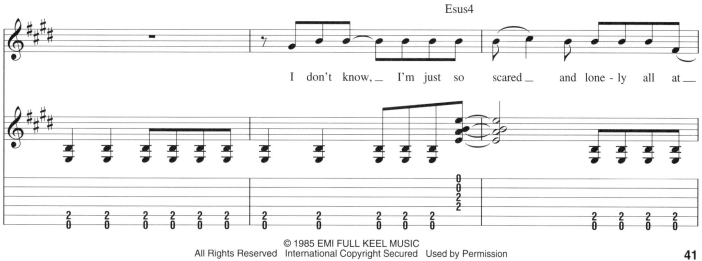

I don't know, __ I'm just so scared __ and lone - ly all at __

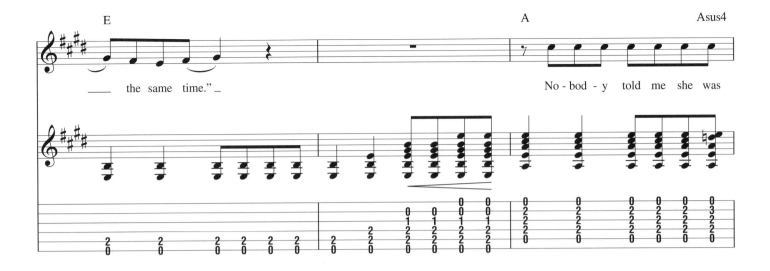

the same time."   No - bod - y told me she was

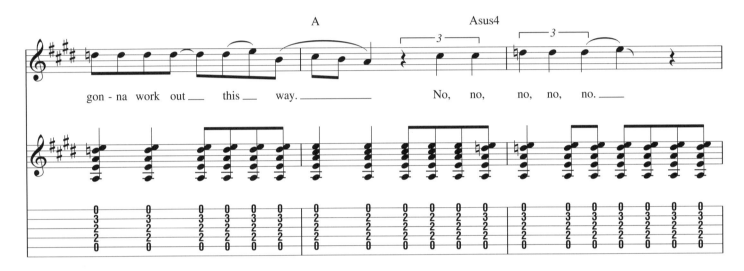

gon - na work out _ this _ way. _   No,   no,   no,   no,   no. _

I guess they knew we'd   work _ it out   in our own _ way. _

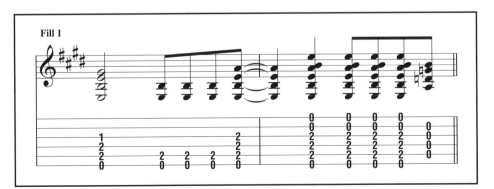

Chorus

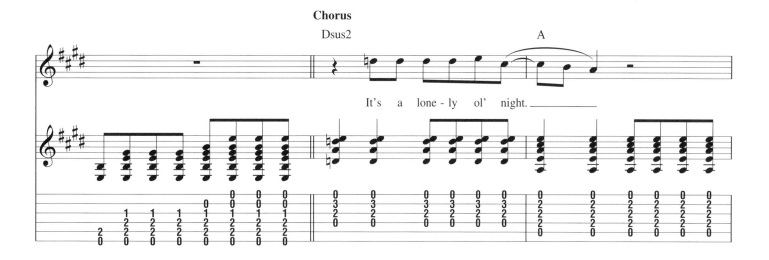

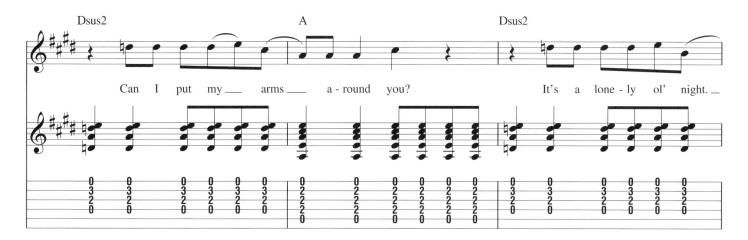

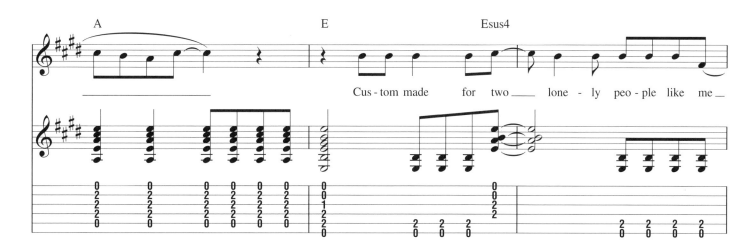

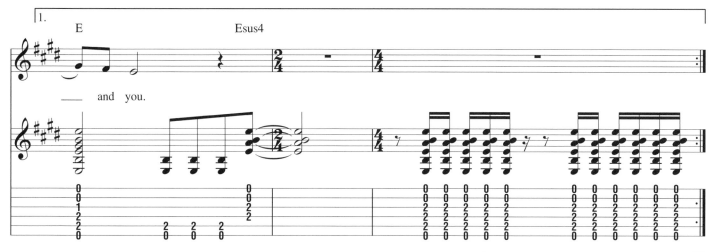

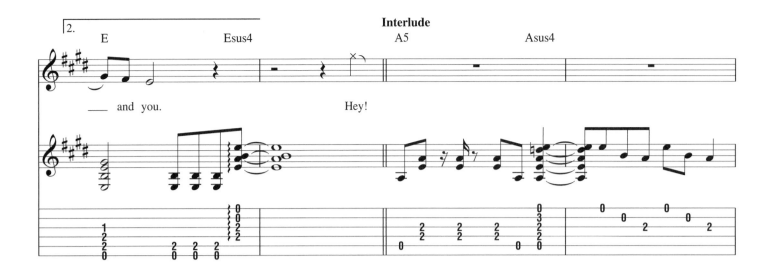

Interlude

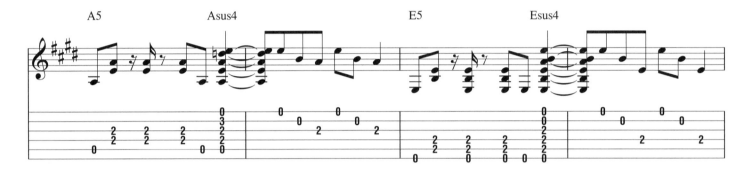

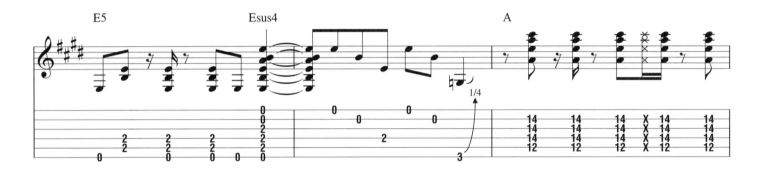

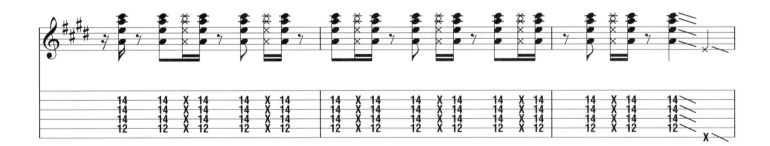

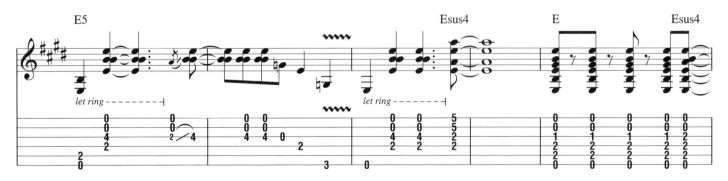

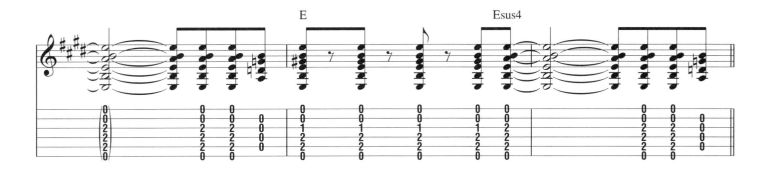

Bridge

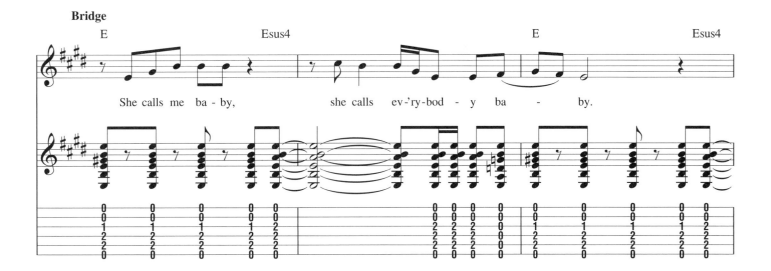

She calls me ba - by,   she calls ev-'ry-bod - y ba - by.

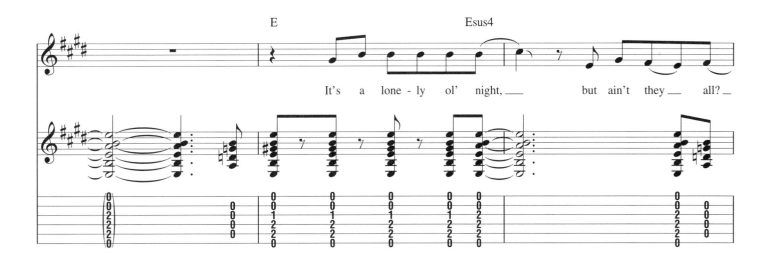

It's a lone - ly ol' night, ___ but ain't they ___ all? ___

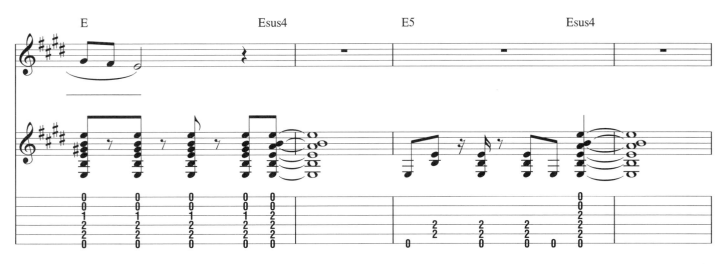

Outro-Chorus

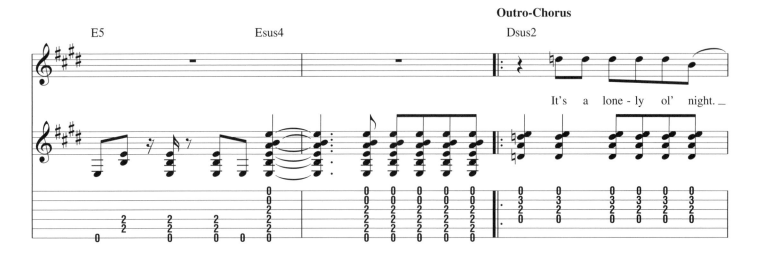

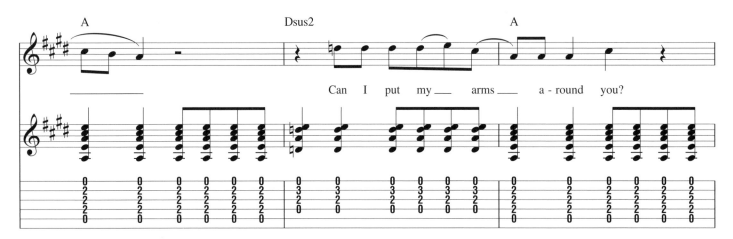

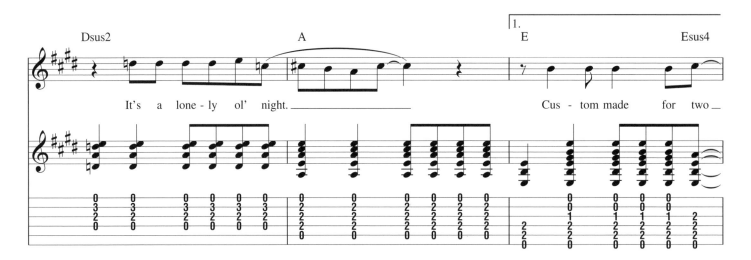

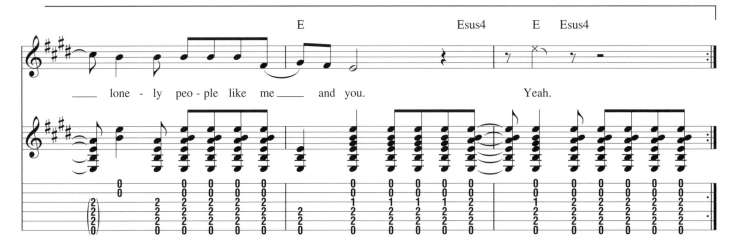

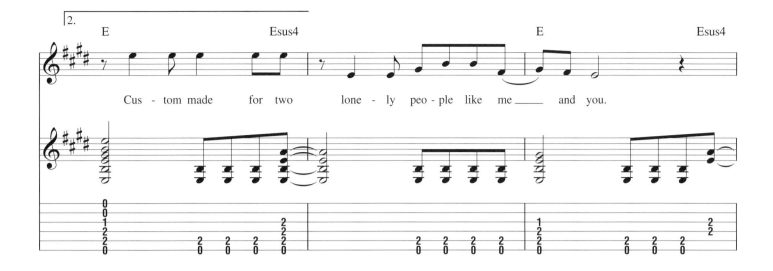

Cus - tom made   for two   lone - ly peo - ple like me ____ and you.

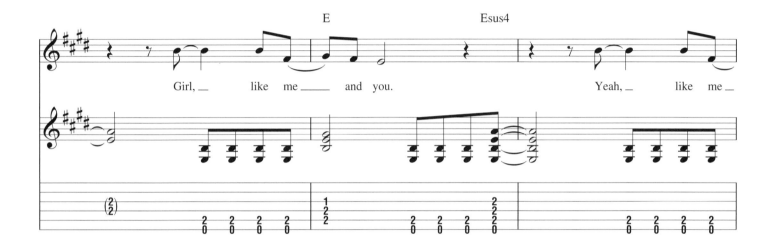

Girl, ___ like me ____ and you.   Yeah, ___ like me __

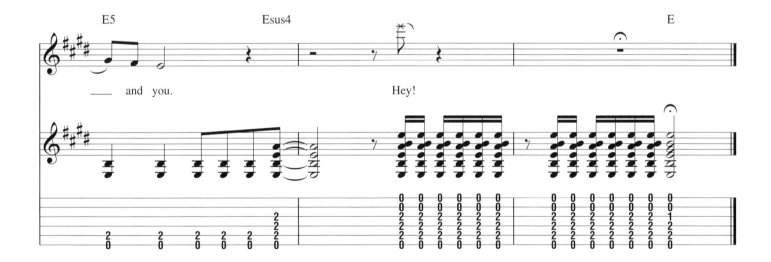

___ and you.   Hey!

Additional Lyrics

2. Radio playin' softly, some singer's sad, sad song.
He's singin' about standin' in the shadows of love,
I guess it feels awfully alone.
She says, "I know exactly what he means."
Yeah, yeah, yeah, yeah, yeah.
And it's a sad, sad, sad, sad feeling
When you're living on those in-betweens.
But it's okay.

Pink Houses

Words and Music by John Mellencamp

Open G tuning:
(low to high) D-G-D-G-B-D

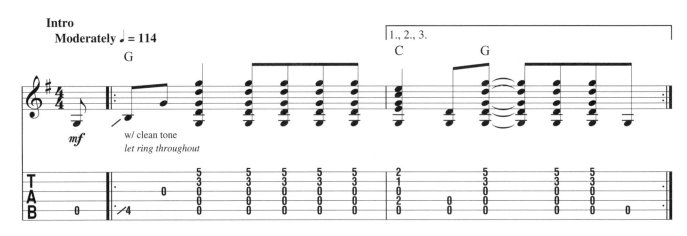

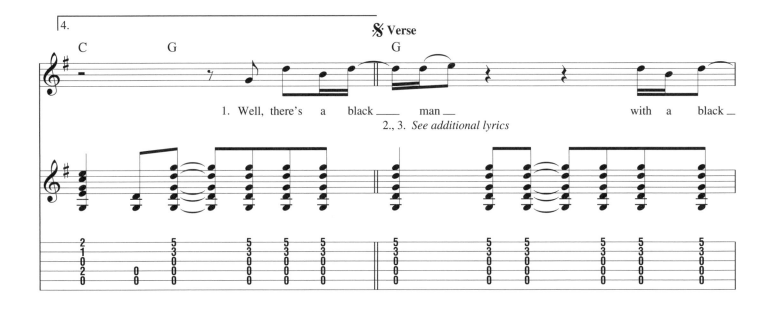

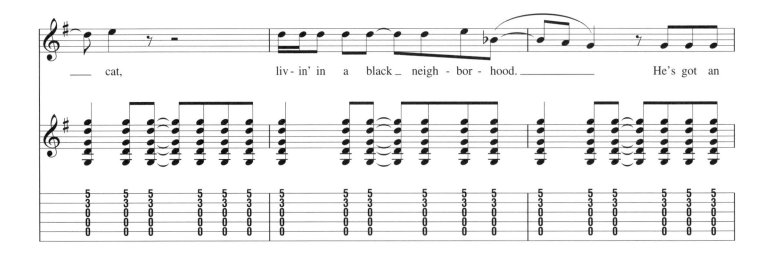

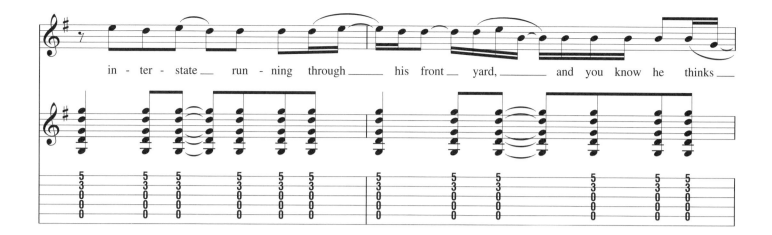

in - ter - state ___ run - ning through _____ his front ___ yard, _____ and you know he thinks ___

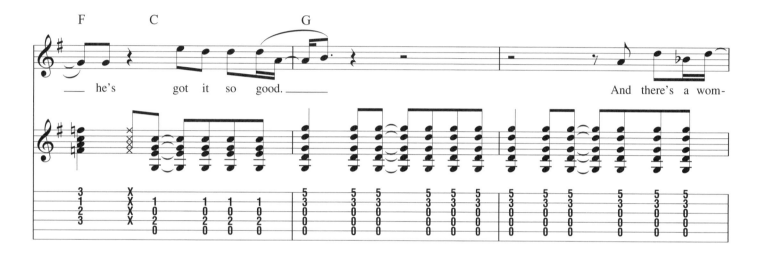

F   C   G

___ he's ___ got it so good. _____   And there's a wom-

- an ___ in the kitch - en, ___   clean-ing up the eve - ning ___ slop. ___

To Coda 1 ⊕
To Coda 2 ⊕
              F   C

___ And he looks ___ at her and ___ says, "Hey dar- lin', I can re - mem- ber when ___ you could ___

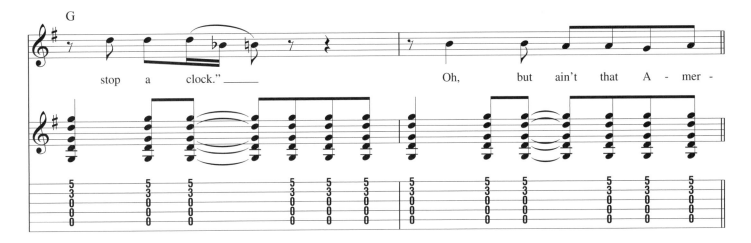

Chorus

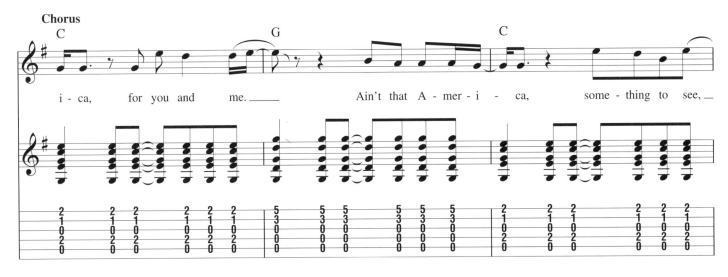

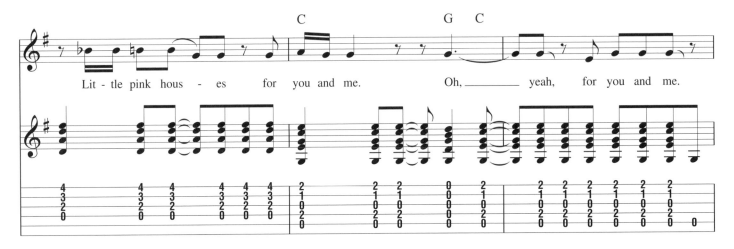

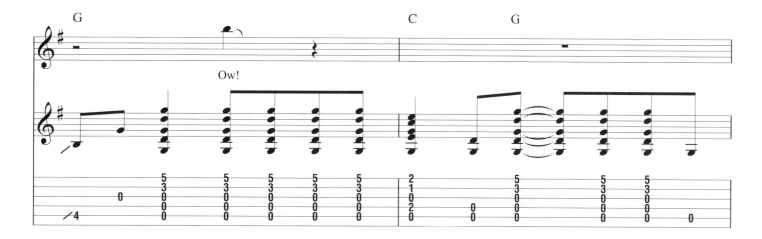

Ow!

D.S. al Coda 1

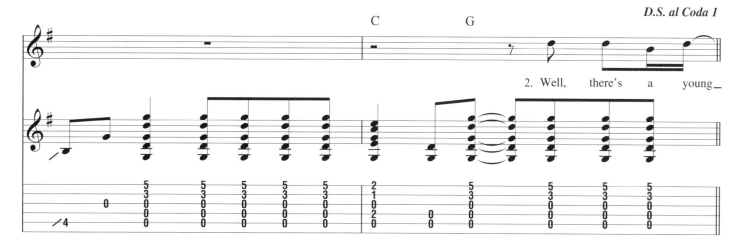

2. Well, there's a young

Coda 1

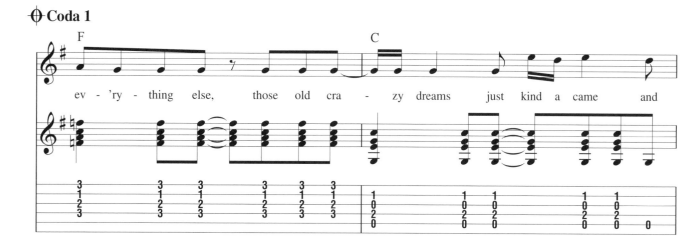

ev - 'ry - thing else, those old cra - zy dreams just kind a came and

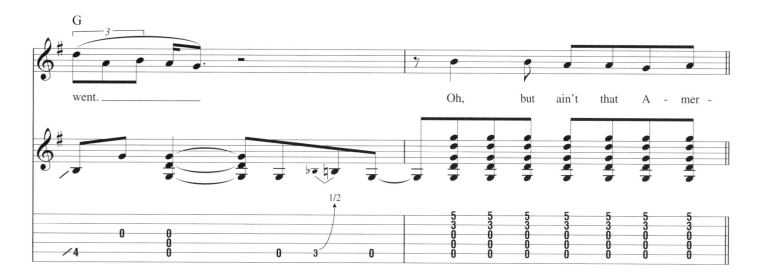

went. _____

Oh, but ain't that A - mer -

Chorus

i - ca, for you and me. ___ Ain't that A - mer - i - ca, some - thing to see, ___

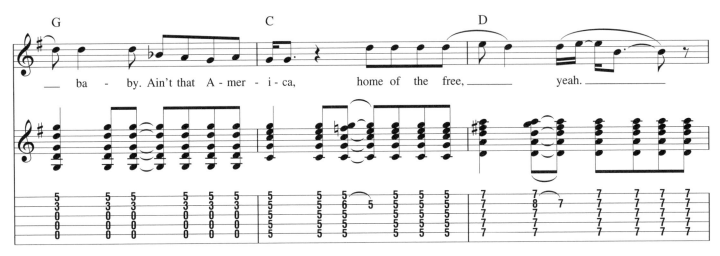

___ ba - by. Ain't that A - mer - i - ca, home of the free, _____ yeah. ___

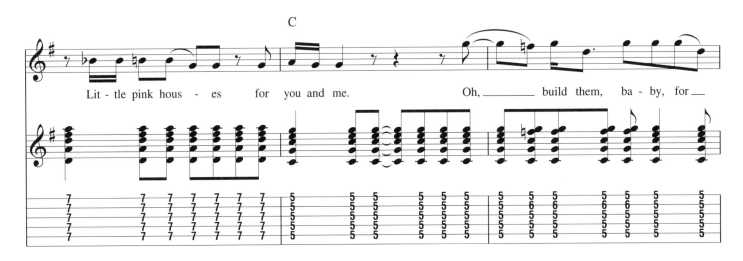

Lit - tle pink hous - es for you and me. Oh, ___ build them, ba - by, for ___

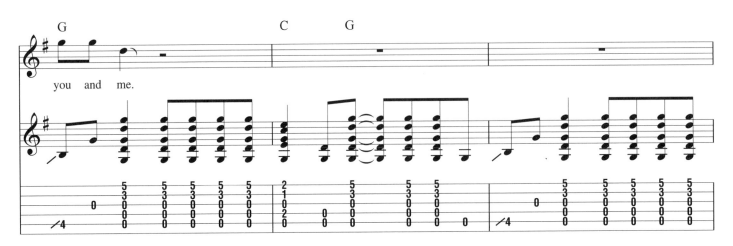

you and me.

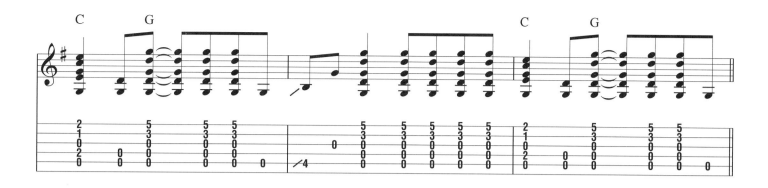

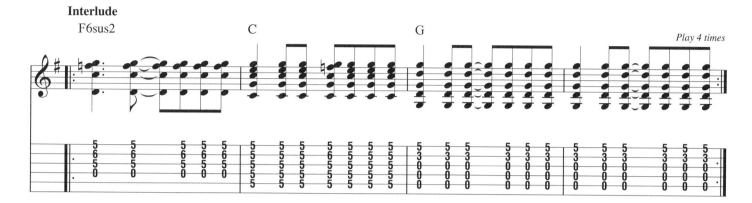

Interlude

Play 4 times

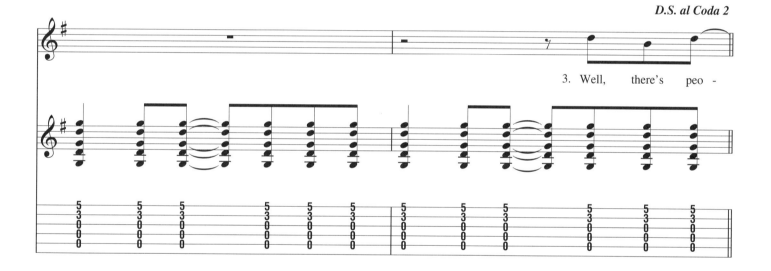

D.S. al Coda 2

3. Well, there's peo -

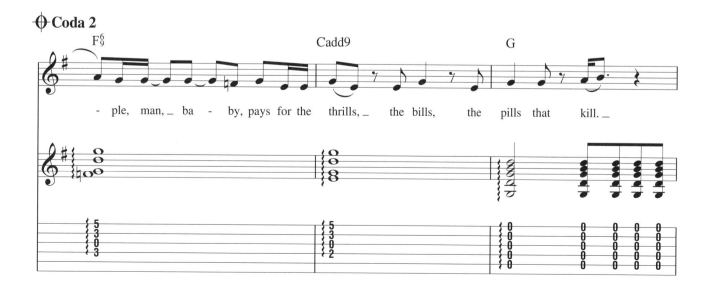

Coda 2

- ple, man, __ ba - by, pays for the thrills, __ the bills, the pills that kill. __

Oh, but ain't that A - mer - i - ca, for you and me.____ Ain't that A - mer -

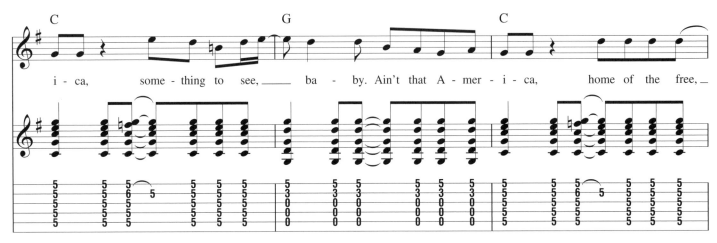

i - ca, some - thing to see,____ ba - by. Ain't that A - mer - i - ca, home of the free, _

{ 1. yeah.____
2. Ooh, yeah, yeah,____ yeah, yeah, yeah, yeah,

Lit - tle pink hous - es for you and me. Ooh. ____

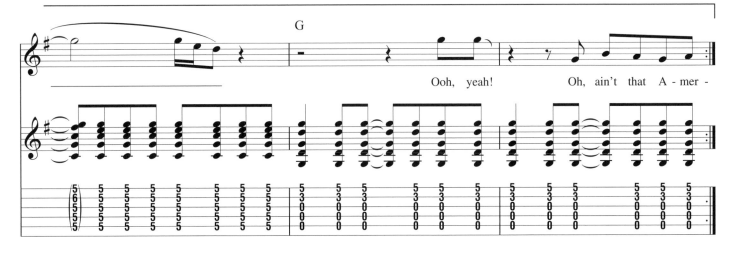

Ooh, yeah! Oh, ain't that A - mer -

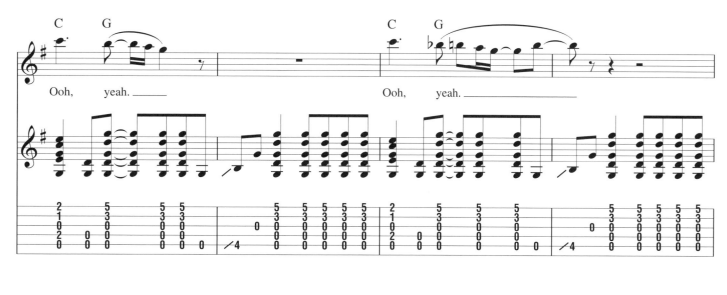

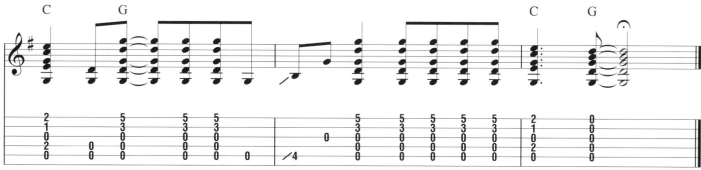

Additional Lyrics

2. Well, there's a young man in a tee-shirt,
   List'nin' to a rock 'n' roller station.
   He's got a greasy hair and a greasy smile.
   He says, "Lord, this must be my destination."
   'Cause they told me when I was younger,
   Sayin', "Boy, you're gonna be president."
   But just like ev'rything else, those old crazy dreams
   Just kinda came and went.

3. Well, there's people, and more people.
   What do they know, know, know?
   Go to work in some high rise
   And vacation down at the Gulf of Mexico, ooh, yeah.
   And there's winners and there's losers,
   But they ain't no big deal.
   'Cause the simple, man, baby, pays for the thrills,
   The bills, the pills that kill.

Small Town

**Words and Music by
John Mellencamp**

Capo IV

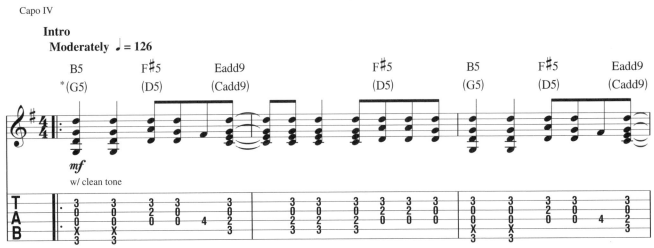

*Symbols in parentheses represent chord names respective to capoed guitar
and do not reflect actual sounding chords. Capoed fret is "0" in tab.

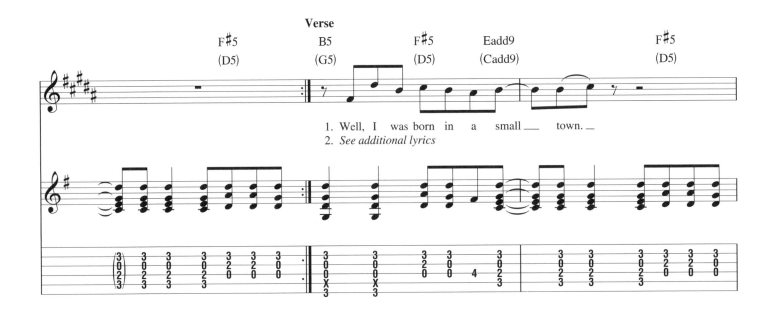

1. Well, I was born in a small ___ town. ___
2. *See additional lyrics*

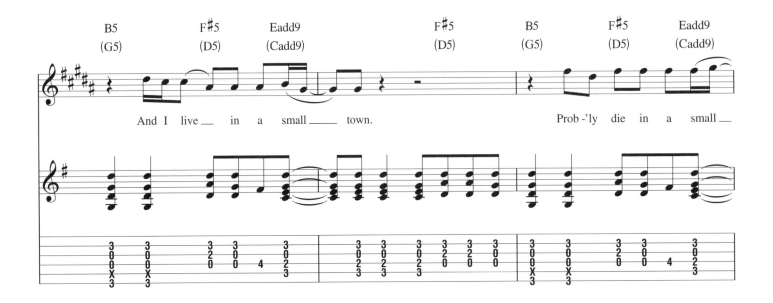

And I live ___ in a small ___ town.   Prob-'ly die in a small ___

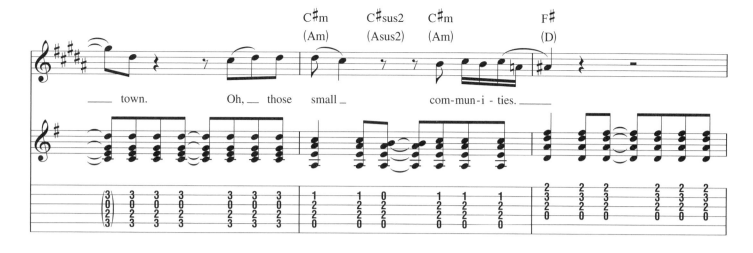

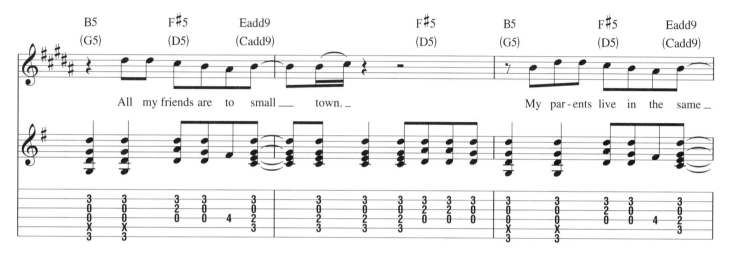

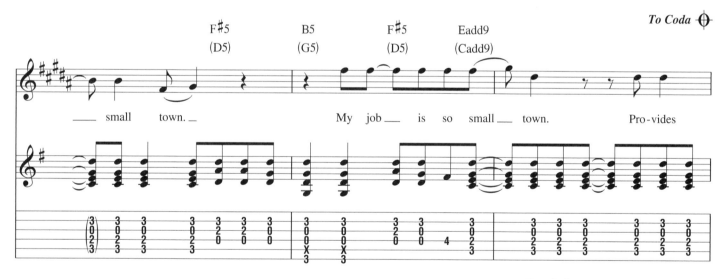

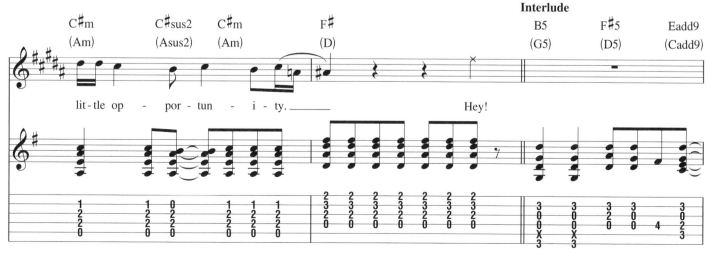

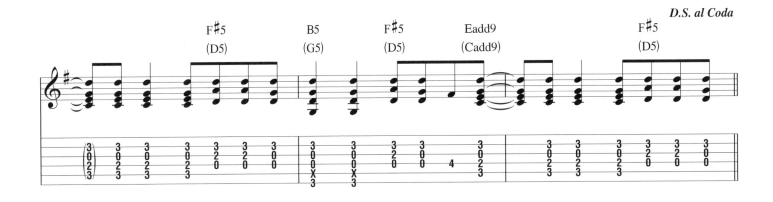

Coda

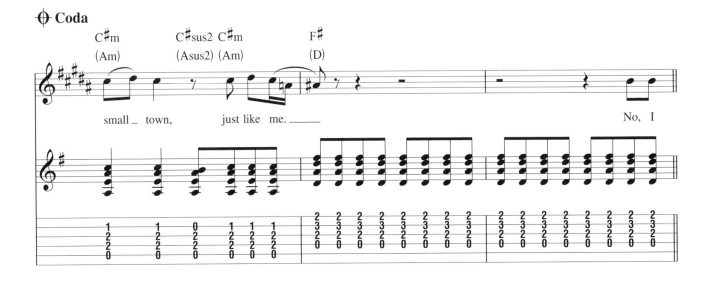

small _ town,   just like me. _____   No, I

Bridge

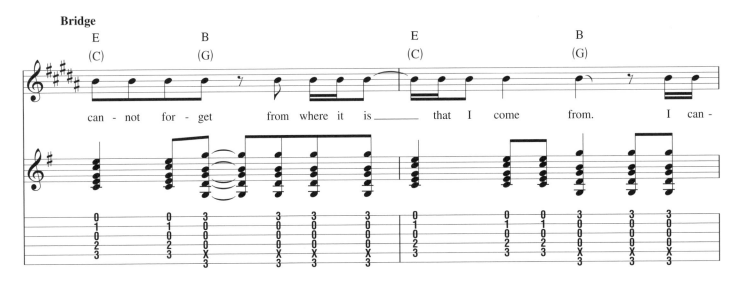

can - not for - get   from where it is _____ that I come from.   I can -

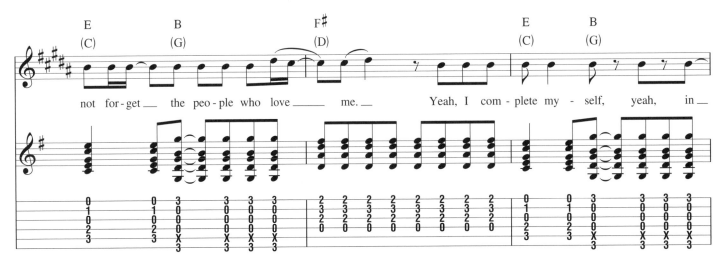

not for - get _ the peo - ple who love _____ me. _____   Yeah, I com - plete my - self, yeah, in

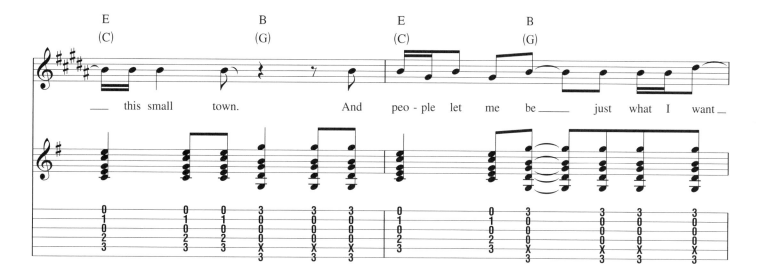

_____ this small town. And peo-ple let me be _____ just what I want _____

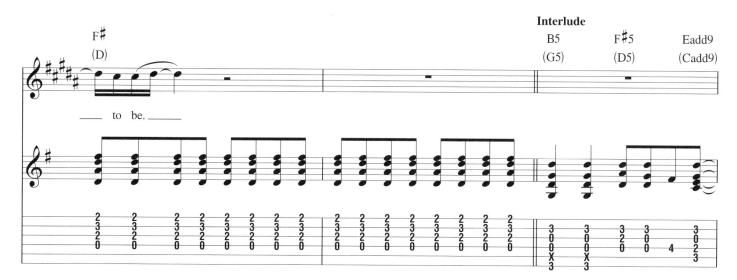

_____ to be. _____

Interlude

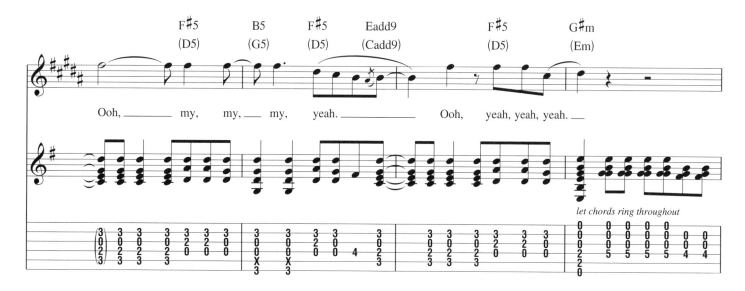

Ooh, _____ my, my, _____ my, yeah. _____ Ooh, yeah, yeah, yeah. _____

let chords ring throughout

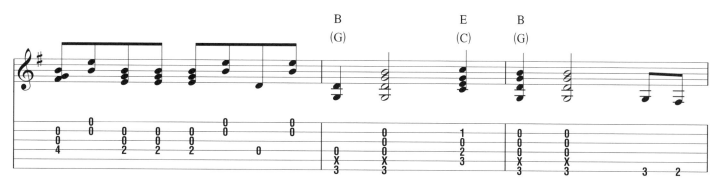

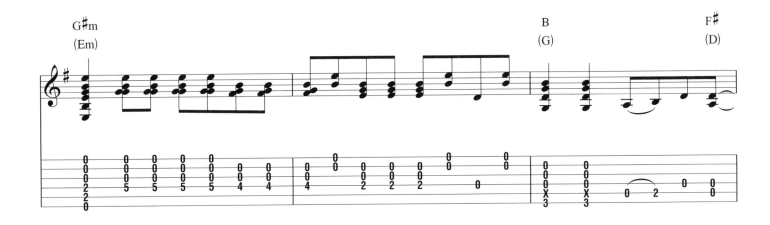

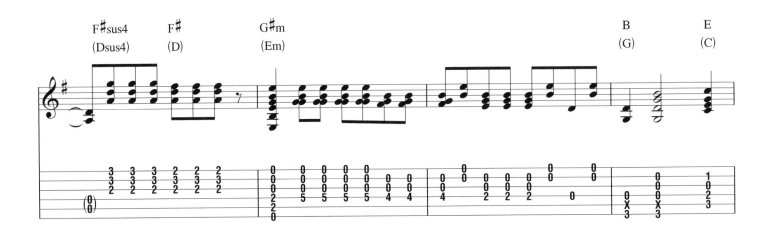

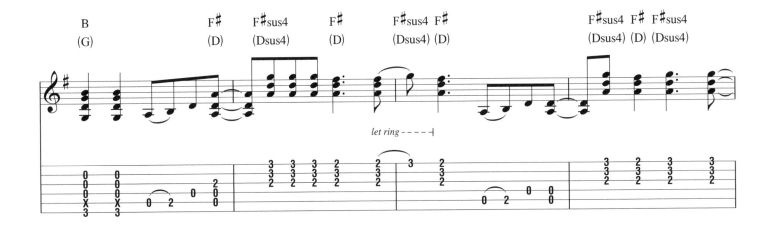

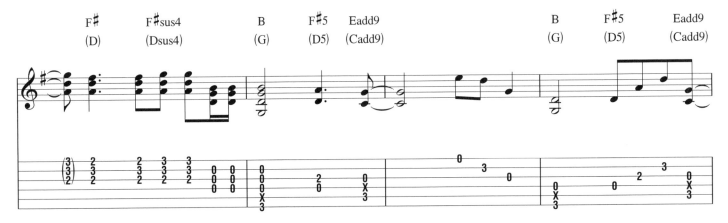

Verse

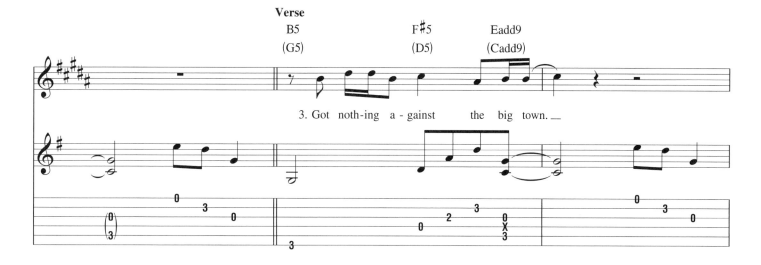

3. Got noth-ing a - gainst the big town. __

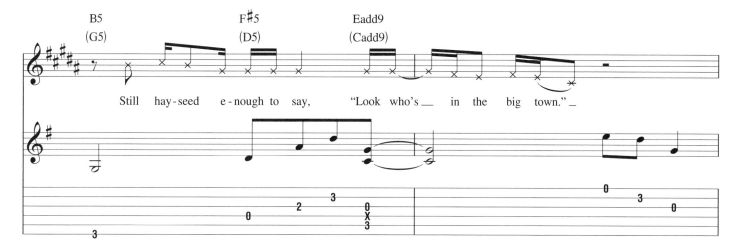

Still hay-seed e - nough to say, "Look who's __ in the big town." __

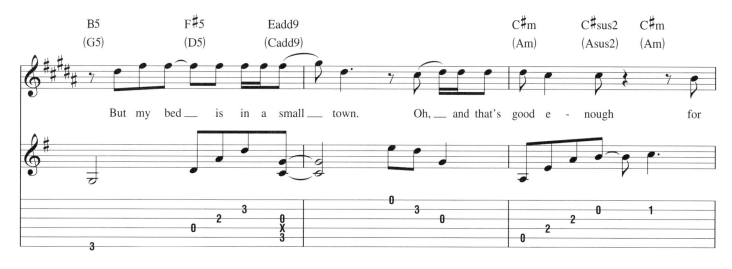

But my bed __ is in a small __ town. Oh, __ and that's good e - nough for

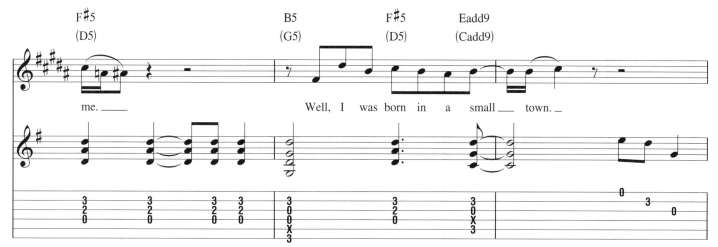

me. __ Well, I was born in a small __ town. __

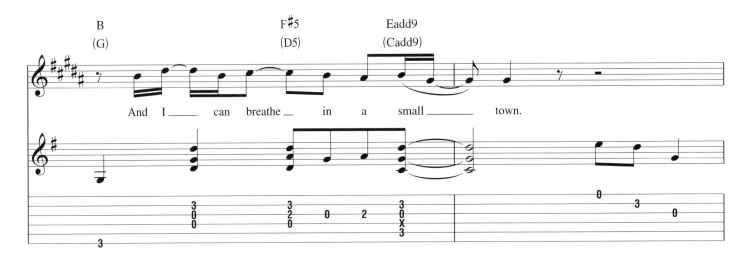

And I ____ can breathe ____ in a small _____ town.

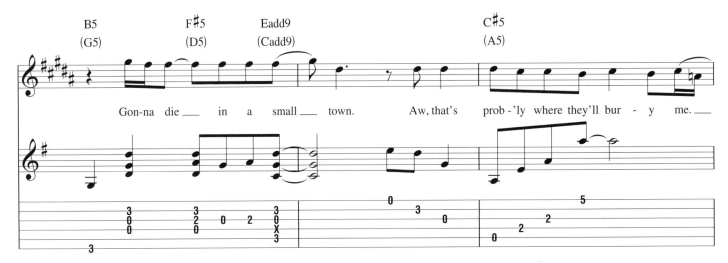

Gon-na die ____ in a small ____ town. Aw, that's prob-'ly where they'll bur-y me. ____

Outro

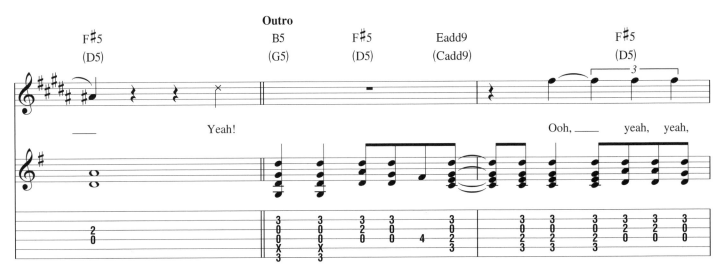

____ Yeah! Ooh, ____ yeah, yeah,

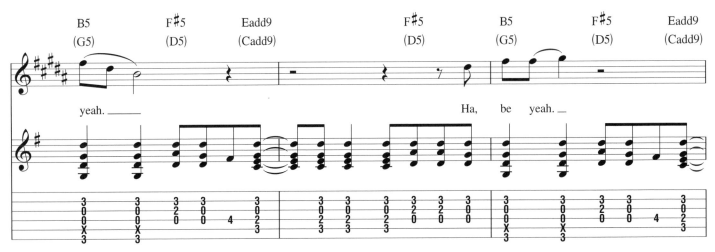

yeah. ____ Ha, be yeah. ____

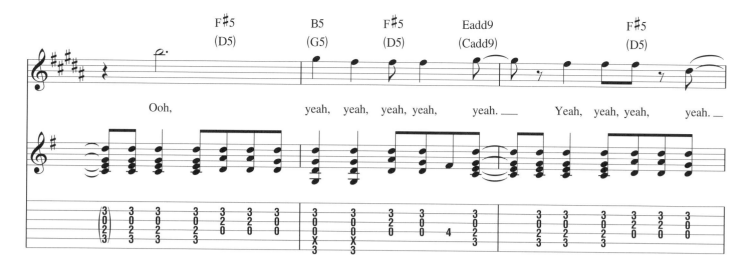

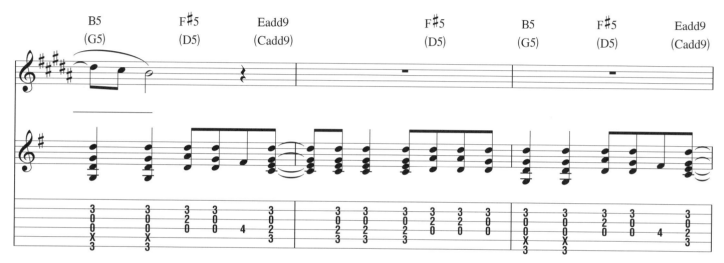

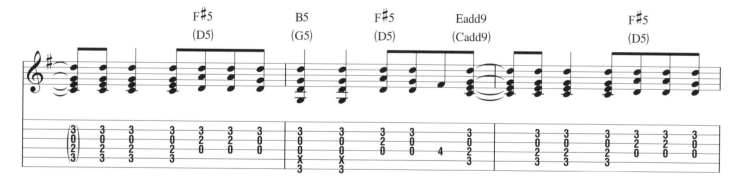

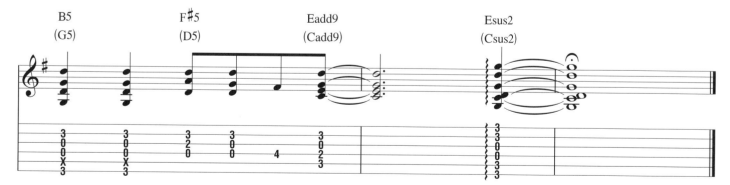

Additional Lyrics

2. Educated in a small town.
   Taught the fear of Jesus in a small town.
   Used to daydream in that small town.
   Another boring romantic, that's me.
   But I've seen it all in a small town.
   Had myself a ball in a small town.
   Married an L.A. doll and brought her to this small town.
   Now she's small town, just like me.

R.O.C.K. in the U.S.A.
(A Salute to 60's Rock)

Words and Music by John Mellencamp

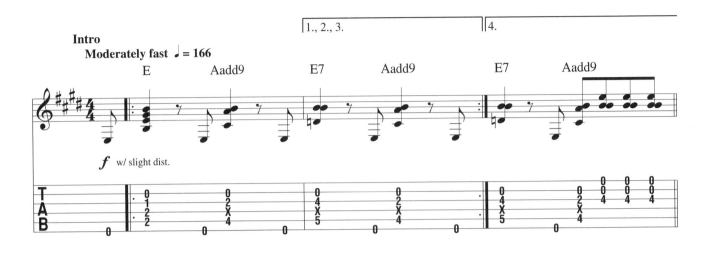

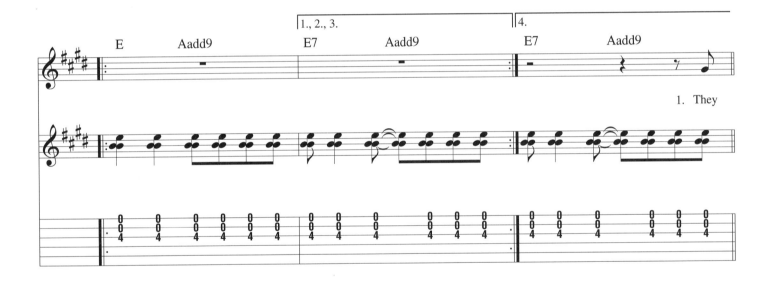

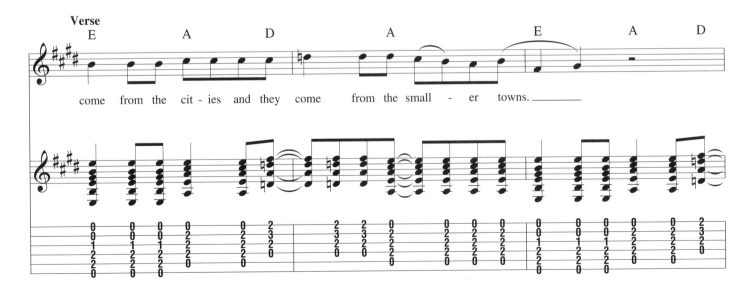

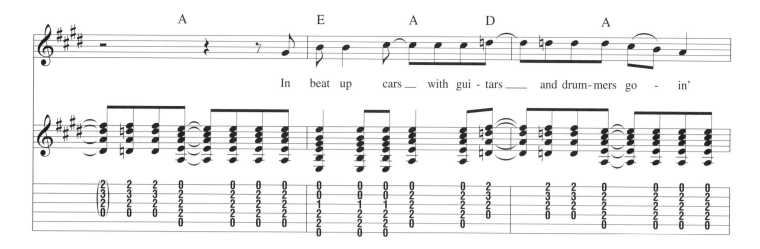

In beat up cars with gui - tars and drum-mers go - in'

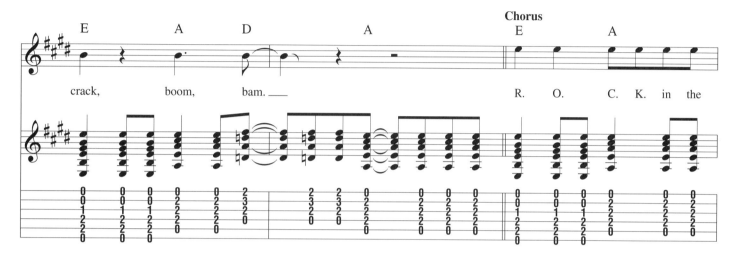

crack, boom, bam. R. O. C. K. in the

Chorus

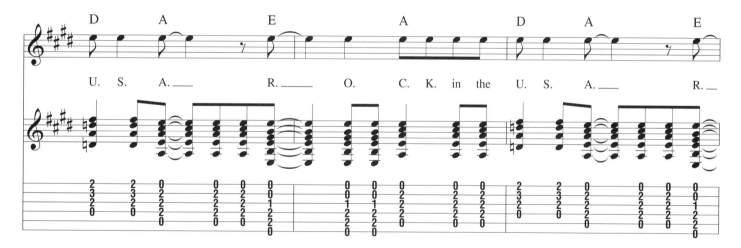

U. S. A. R. O. C. K. in the U. S. A. R.

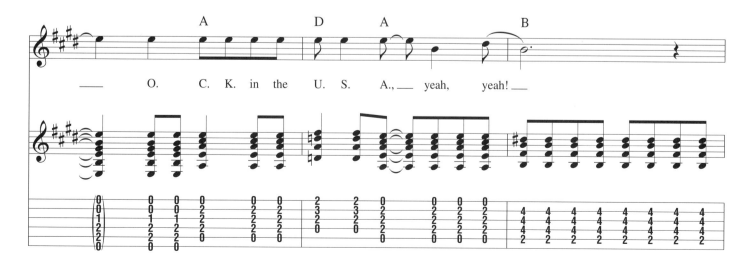

O. C. K. in the U. S. A., yeah, yeah!

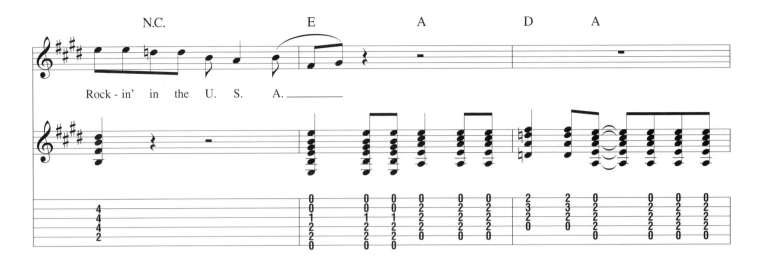

Rock - in' in the U. S. A.

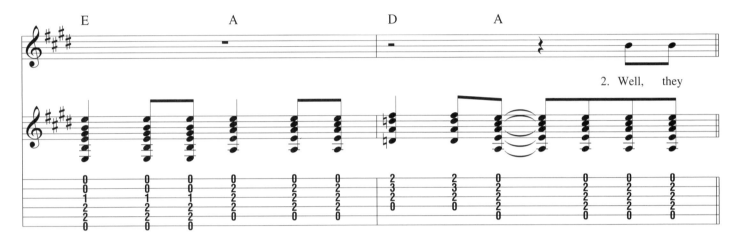

2. Well, they

Verse

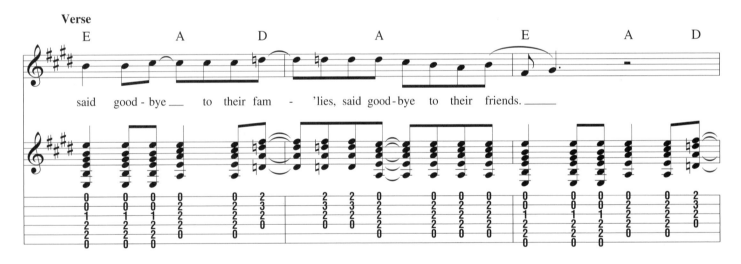

said good-bye ____ to their fam - 'lies, said good-bye to their friends. ____

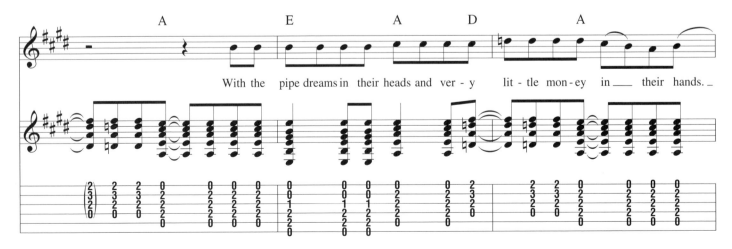

With the pipe dreams in their heads and ver - y lit - tle mon-ey in ____ their hands. ____

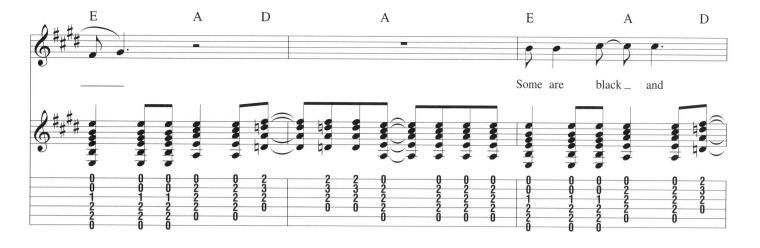

Some are black _ and

some are white _ and they ain't too proud to sleep on your floor _ to - night. _ With the

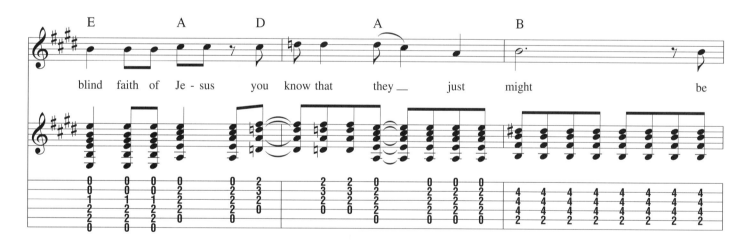

blind faith of Je - sus you know that they _ just might be

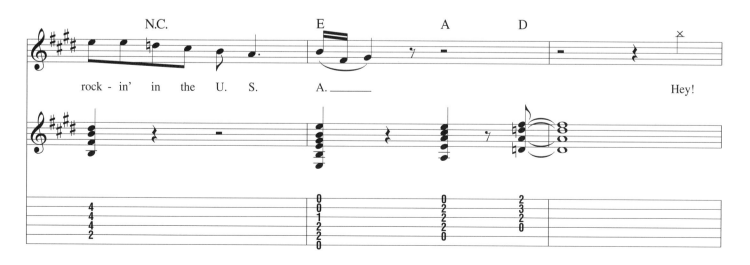

rock - in' in the U. S. A. _ Hey!

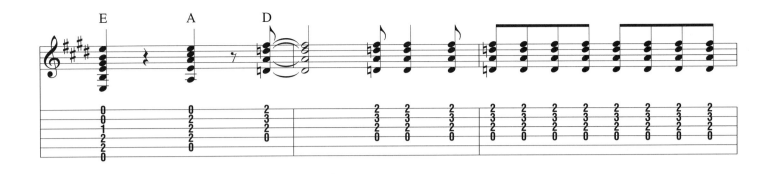

Recorder Solo

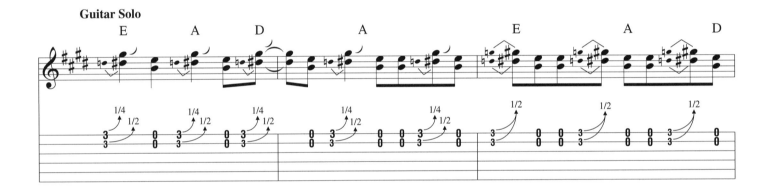

Guitar Solo

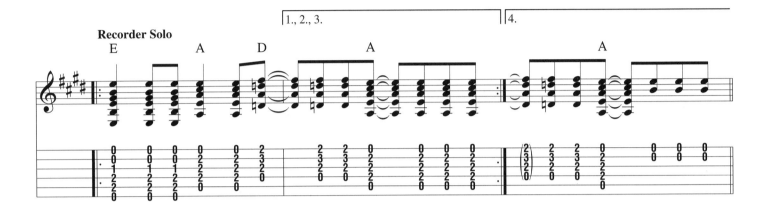

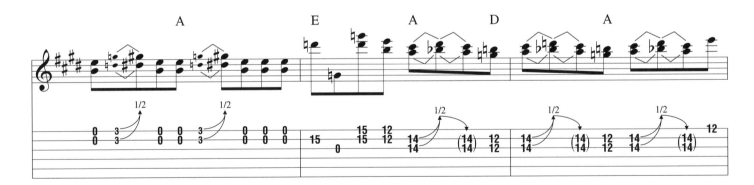

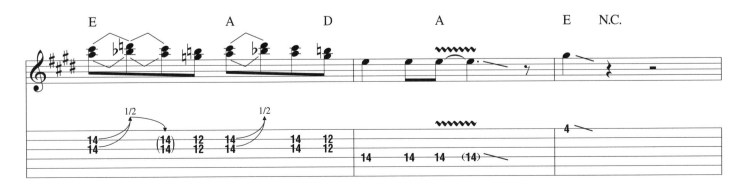

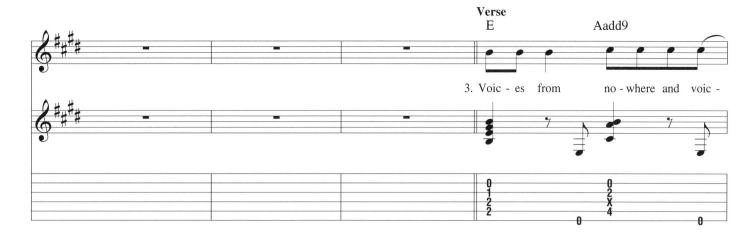

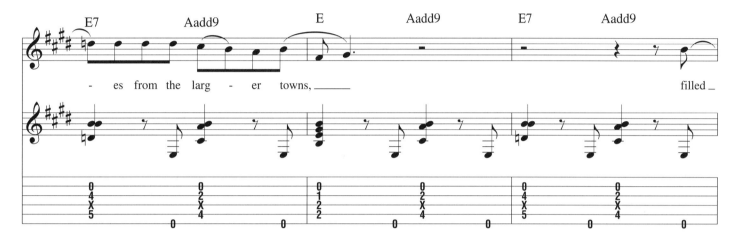

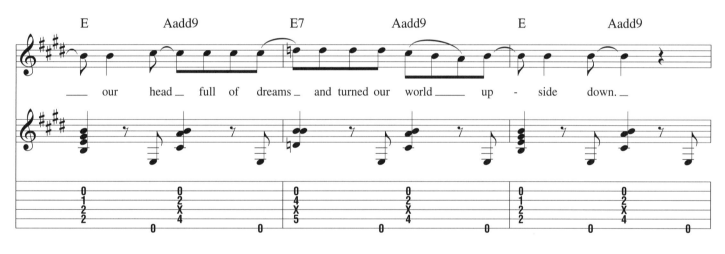

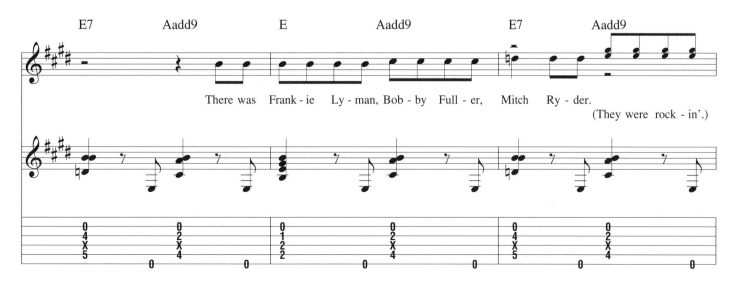

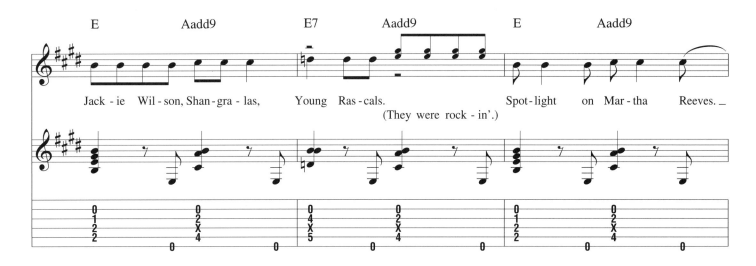

Jack-ie Wil-son, Shan-gra-las, Young Ras-cals. Spot-light on Mar-tha Reeves.
(They were rock-in'.)

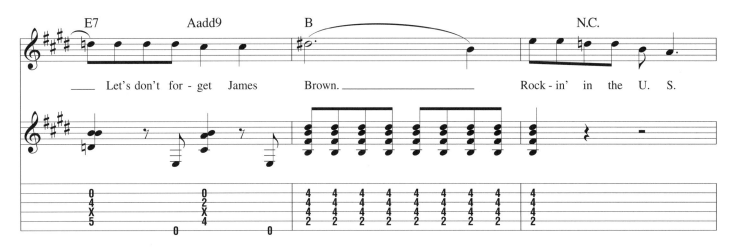

_____ Let's don't for-get James Brown. _____ Rock-in' in the U. S.

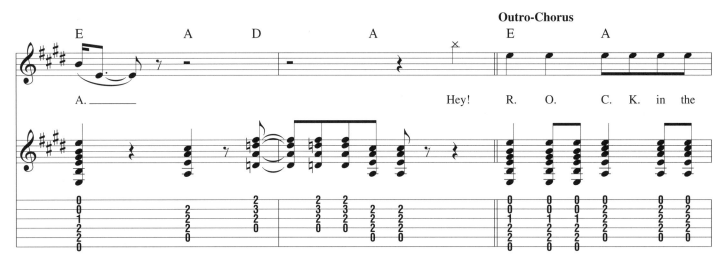

Outro-Chorus

A. _____ Hey! R. O. C. K. in the

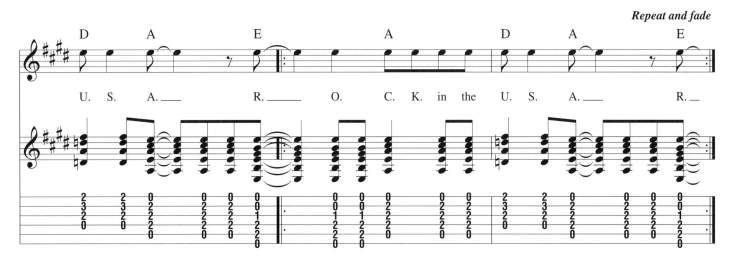

Repeat and fade

U. S. A. _____ R. _____ O. C. K. in the U. S. A. _____ R. _____

GUITAR PLAY-ALONG
Hal Leonard

This series will help you play your favorite songs quickly and easily. Just follow the tab and listen to the CD to hear how the guitar should sound, and then play along using the separate backing tracks. Mac or PC users can also slow down the tempo without changing pitch by using the CD in their computer. The melody and lyrics are included in the book so that you can sing or simply follow along.

1. ROCK
Day Tripper • Message in a Bottle • Refuge • Shattered • Sunshine of Your Love • Takin' Care of Business • Tush • Walk This Way.
00699570 ....$16.99

2. ACOUSTIC
Angie • Behind Blue Eyes • Best of My Love • Blackbird • Dust in the Wind • Layla • Night Moves • Yesterday.
00699569.......................................$16.95

3. HARD ROCK
Crazy Train • Iron Man • Living After Midnight • Rock You like a Hurricane • Round and Round • Smoke on the Water • Sweet Child o' Mine • You Really Got Me.
00699573.......................................$16.95

4. POP/ROCK
Breakdown • Crazy Little Thing Called Love • Hit Me with Your Best Shot • I Want You to Want Me • Lights • R.O.C.K. in the U.S.A. • Summer of '69 • What I Like About You.
00699571.......................................$16.99

5. MODERN ROCK
Aerials • Alive • Bother • Chop Suey! • Control • Last Resort • Take a Look Around (Theme from *M:I-2*) • Wish You Were Here.
00699574 ....$16.99

6. '90s ROCK
Are You Gonna Go My Way • Come out and Play • I'll Stick Around • Know Your Enemy • Man in the Box • Outshined • Smells like Teen Spirit • Under the Bridge.
00699572.......................................$16.99

7. BLUES
All Your Love (I Miss Loving) • Born Under a Bad Sign • Hide Away • I'm Tore Down • I'm Your Hoochie Coochie Man • Pride and Joy • Sweet Home Chicago • The Thrill Is Gone.
00699575.......................................$16.95

8. ROCK
All Right Now • Black Magic Woman • Get Back • Hey Joe • Layla • Love Me Two Times • Won't Get Fooled Again • You Really Got Me.
00699585.......................................$14.95

9. PUNK ROCK
All the Small Things • Fat Lip • Flavor of the Weak • I Feel So • Lifestyles of the Rich and Famous • Say It Ain't So • Self Esteem • (So) Tired of Waiting for You.
00699576.......................................$14.95

10. ACOUSTIC
Here Comes the Sun • Landslide • The Magic Bus • Norwegian Wood (This Bird Has Flown) • Pink Houses • Space Oddity • Tangled Up in Blue • Tears in Heaven.
00699586.......................................$16.95

11. EARLY ROCK
Fun, Fun, Fun • Hound Dog • Louie, Louie • No Particular Place to Go • Oh, Pretty Woman • Rock Around the Clock • Under the Boardwalk • Wild Thing.
0699579.......................................$14.95

12. POP/ROCK
867-5309/Jenny • Every Breath You Take • Money for Nothing • Rebel, Rebel • Run to You • Ticket to Ride • Wonderful Tonight • You Give Love a Bad Name.
00699587.......................................$14.95

13. FOLK ROCK
Annie's Song • Leaving on a Jet Plane • Suite: Judy Blue Eyes • This Land Is Your Land • Time in a Bottle • Turn! Turn! Turn! • You've Got a Friend • You've Got to Hide Your Love Away.
00699581.......................................$14.95

14. BLUES ROCK
Blue on Black • Crossfire • Cross Road Blues (Crossroads) • The House Is Rockin' • La Grange • Move It on Over • Roadhouse Blues • Statesboro Blues.
00699582.......................................$16.95

15. R&B
Ain't Too Proud to Beg • Brick House • Get Ready • I Can't Help Myself • I Got You (I Feel Good) • I Heard It Through the Grapevine • My Girl • Shining Star.
00699583.......................................$14.95

16. JAZZ
All Blues • Bluesette • Footprints • How Insensitive • Misty • Satin Doll • Stella by Starlight • Tenor Madness.
00699584.......................................$15.95

17. COUNTRY
Amie • Boot Scootin' Boogie • Chattahoochee • Folsom Prison Blues • Friends in Low Places • Forever and Ever, Amen • T-R-O-U-B-L-E • Workin' Man Blues.
00699588.......................................$15.95

18. ACOUSTIC ROCK
About a Girl • Breaking the Girl • Drive • Iris • More than Words • Patience • Silent Lucidity • 3 AM.
00699577.......................................$15.95

19. SOUL
Get Up (I Feel like Being) a Sex Machine • Green Onions • In the Midnight Hour • Knock on Wood • Mustang Sally • Respect • (Sittin' On) The Dock of the Bay • Soul Man.
00699578.......................................$14.95

20. ROCKABILLY
Be-Bop-A-Lula • Blue Suede Shoes • Hello Mary Lou • Little Sister • Mystery Train • Rock This Town • Stray Cat Strut • That'll Be the Day.
00699580.......................................$14.95

21. YULETIDE
Angels We Have Heard on High • Away in a Manger • Deck the Hall • The First Noel • Go, Tell It on the Mountain • Jingle Bells • Joy to the World • O Little Town of Bethlehem.
00699602.......................................$14.95

22. CHRISTMAS
The Christmas Song • Frosty the Snow Man • Happy Xmas • Here Comes Santa Claus • Jingle-Bell Rock • Merry Christmas, Darling • Rudolph the Red-Nosed Reindeer • Silver Bells.
00699600.......................................$15.95

23. SURF
Let's Go Trippin' • Out of Limits • Penetration • Pipeline • Surf City • Surfin' U.S.A. • Walk Don't Run • The Wedge.
00699635.......................................$14.95

24. ERIC CLAPTON
Badge • Bell Bottom Blues • Change the World • Cocaine • Key to the Highway • Lay Down Sally • White Room • Wonderful Tonight.
00699649.......................................$16.95

25. LENNON & McCARTNEY
Back in the U.S.S.R. • Drive My Car • Get Back • A Hard Day's Night • I Feel Fine • Paperback Writer • Revolution • Ticket to Ride.
00699642 ....$14.95

26. ELVIS PRESLEY
All Shook Up • Blue Suede Shoes • Don't Be Cruel • Heartbreak Hotel • Hound Dog • Jailhouse Rock • Little Sister • Mystery Train.
00699643.......................................$14.95

27. DAVID LEE ROTH
Ain't Talkin' 'bout Love • Dance the Night Away • Hot for Teacher • Just like Paradise • A Lil' Ain't Enough • Runnin' with the Devil • Unchained • Yankee Rose.
00699645.......................................$16.95

28. GREG KOCH
Chief's Blues • Death of a Bassman • Dylan the Villain • The Grip • Holy Grail • Spank It • Tonus Diabolicus • Zoiks.
00699646.......................................$14.95

29. BOB SEGER
Against the Wind • Betty Lou's Gettin' out Tonight • Hollywood Nights • Mainstreet • Night Moves • Old Time Rock & Roll • Rock and Roll Never Forgets • Still the Same.
00699647.......................................$14.95

30. KISS
Cold Gin • Detroit Rock City • Deuce • Firehouse • Heaven's on Fire • Love Gun • Rock and Roll All Nite • Shock Me.
00699644.......................................$14.95

31. CHRISTMAS HITS
Blue Christmas • Do You Hear What I Hear • Happy Holiday • I Saw Mommy Kissing Santa Claus • I'll Be Home for Christmas • Let It Snow! Let It Snow! Let It Snow! • Little Saint Nick • Snowfall.
00699652.......................................$14.95

32. THE OFFSPRING
Bad Habit • Come out and Play • Gone Away • Gotta Get Away • Hit That • The Kids Aren't Alright • Pretty Fly (For a White Guy) • Self Esteem.
00699653.......................................$14.95

33. ACOUSTIC CLASSICS
Across the Universe • Babe, I'm Gonna Leave You • Crazy on You • Heart of Gold • Hotel California • I'd Love to Change the World • Thick as a Brick • Wanted Dead or Alive.
00699656.......................................$16.95

34. CLASSIC ROCK
Aqualung • Born to Be Wild • The Boys Are Back in Town • Brown Eyed Girl • Reeling in the Years • Rock'n Me • Rocky Mountain Way • Sweet Emotion.
00699658.......................................$16.95

35. HAIR METAL
Decadence Dance • Don't Treat Me Bad • Down Boys • Seventeen • Shake Me • Up All Night • Wait • Talk Dirty to Me.
00699660.......................................$16.95

36. SOUTHERN ROCK
Can't You See • Flirtin' with Disaster • Hold on Loosely • Jessica • Mississippi Queen • Ramblin' Man • Sweet Home Alabama • What's Your Name.
00699661.......................................$16.95

37. ACOUSTIC METAL
Every Rose Has Its Thorn • Fly to the Angels • Hole Hearted • Love Is on the Way • Love of a Lifetime • Signs • To Be with You • When the Children Cry.
00699662.......................................$16.95

38. BLUES
Boom Boom • Cold Shot • Crosscut Saw • Everyday I Have the Blues • Frosty • Further on up the Road • Killing Floor • Texas Flood.
00699663.......................................$16.95

39. '80s METAL
Bark at the Moon • Big City Nights • Breaking the Chains • Cult of Personality • Lay It Down • Living on a Prayer • Panama • Smokin' in the Boys Room.
00699664.......................................$16.99

40. INCUBUS
Are You In? • Drive • Megalomaniac • Nice to Know You • Pardon Me • Stellar • Talk Shows on Mute • Wish You Were Here.
00699668.......................................$17.95

41. ERIC CLAPTON
After Midnight • Can't Find My Way Home • Forever Man • I Shot the Sheriff • I'm Tore Down • Pretending • Running on Faith • Tears in Heaven.
00699669.......................................$16.95

42. CHART HITS
Are You Gonna Be My Girl • Heaven • Here Without You • I Believe in a Thing Called Love • Just like You • Last Train Home • This Love • Until the Day I Die.
00699670.......................................$16.95

43. LYNYRD SKYNYRD
Don't Ask Me No Questions • Free Bird • Gimme Three Steps • I Know a Little • Saturday Night Special • Sweet Home Alabama • That Smell • You Got That Right.
00699681.......................................$17.95

44. JAZZ
I Remember You • I'll Remember April • Impressions • In a Mellow Tone • Moonlight in Vermont • On a Slow Boat to China • Things Ain't What They Used to Be • Yesterdays.
00699689........................$14.95

45. TV THEMES
Themes from shows such as: The Addams Family • Hawaii Five-O • King of the Hill • Charlie Brown • Mission: Impossible • The Munsters • The Simpsons • Star Trek®.
00699718........................$14.95

46. MAINSTREAM ROCK
Just a Girl • Keep Away • Kryptonite • Lightning Crashes • 1979 • One Step Closer • Scar Tissue • Torn.
00699722........................$16.95

47. HENDRIX SMASH HITS
All Along the Watchtower • Can You See Me? • Crosstown Traffic • Fire • Foxey Lady • Hey Joe • Manic Depression • Purple Haze • Red House • Remember • Stone Free • The Wind Cries Mary.
00699723........................$19.95

48. AEROSMITH CLASSICS
Back in the Saddle • Draw the Line • Dream On • Last Child • Mama Kin • Same Old Song & Dance • Sweet Emotion • Walk This Way.
00699724........................$16.99

49. STEVIE RAY VAUGHAN
Couldn't Stand the Weather • Empty Arms • Lenny • Little Wing • Look at Little Sister • Love Struck Baby • The Sky Is Crying • Tightrope.
00699725........................$16.95

50. NÜ METAL
Duality • Here to Stay • In the End • Judith • Nookie • So Cold • Toxicity • Whatever.
00699726........................$14.95

51. ALTERNATIVE '90s
Alive • Cherub Rock • Come As You Are • Give It Away • Jane Says • No Excuses • No Rain • Santeria.
00699727........................$12.95

52. FUNK
Cissy Strut • Flashlight • Funk #49 • I Just Want to Celebrate • It's Your Thing • Le Freak • Papa's Got a Brand New Bag • Pick up the Pieces.
00699728........................$14.95

54. HEAVY METAL
Am I Evil? • Back in Black • Holy Diver • Lights Out • The Trooper • You've Got Another Thing Comin' • The Zoo.
00699730........................$14.95

55. POP METAL
Beautiful Girls • Cherry Pie • Get the Funk Out • Here I Go Again • Nothin' but a Good Time • Photograph • Turn up the Radio • We're Not Gonna Take It.
00699731........................$14.95

56. FOO FIGHTERS
All My Life • Best of You • DOA • I'll Stick Around • Learn to Fly • Monkey Wrench • My Hero • This Is a Call.
00699749........................$14.95

57. SYSTEM OF A DOWN
Aerials • B.Y.O.B. • Chop Suey! • Innervision • Question! • Spiders • Sugar • Toxicity.
00699751........................$14.95

58. BLINK-182
Adam's Song • All the Small Things • Dammit • Feeling This • Man Overboard • The Rock Show • Stay Together for the Kids • What's My Age Again?
00699772........................$14.95

59. GODSMACK
Awake • Bad Religion • Greed • I Stand Alone • Keep Away • Running Blind • Straight out of Line • Whatever.
00699773........................$14.95

60. 3 DOORS DOWN
Away from the Sun • Duck and Run • Here Without You • Kryptonite • Let Me Go • Live for Today • Loser • When I'm Gone.
00699774........................$14.95

61. SLIPKNOT
Before I Forget • Duality • The Heretic Anthem • Left Behind • My Plague • Spit It Out • Vermilion • Wait and Bleed.
00699775........................$14.95

62. CHRISTMAS CAROLS
God Rest Ye Merry, Gentlemen • Hark! The Herald Angels Sing • It Came upon the Midnight Clear • O Come, All Ye Faithful (Adeste Fideles) • O Holy Night • Silent Night • We Three Kings of Orient Are • What Child Is This?
00699798........................$12.95

63. CREEDENCE CLEARWATER REVIVAL
Bad Moon Rising • Born on the Bayou • Down on the Corner • Fortunate Son • Green River • Lodi • Proud Mary • Up Around the Bend.
00699802........................$16.99

64. OZZY OSBOURNE
Bark at the Moon • Crazy Train • Flying High Again • Miracle Man • Mr. Crowley • No More Tears • Rock 'N Roll Rebel • Shot in the Dark.
00699803........................$16.99

65. THE DOORS
Break on Through to the Other Side • Hello, I Love You (Won't You Tell Me Your Name?) • L.A. Woman • Light My Fire • Love Me Two Times • People Are Strange • Riders on the Storm • Roadhouse Blues.
00699806........................$16.99

66. THE ROLLING STONES
Beast of Burden • Happy • It's Only Rock 'N' Roll (But I Like It) • Miss You • Shattered • She's So Cold • Start Me Up • Tumbling Dice.
00699807........................$16.95

67. BLACK SABBATH
Black Sabbath • Children of the Grave • Iron Man • N.I.B. • Paranoid • Sabbath, Bloody Sabbath • Sweet Leaf • War Pigs (Interpolating Luke's Wall).
00699808........................$16.99

68. PINK FLOYD – DARK SIDE OF THE MOON
Any Colour You Like • Brain Damage • Breathe • Eclipse • Money • Time • Us and Them.
00699809........................$16.99

69. ACOUSTIC FAVORITES
Against the Wind • Band on the Run • Free Fallin' • Have You Ever Seen the Rain? • Love the One You're With • Maggie May • Melissa • Mrs. Robinson.
00699810........................$14.95

71. CHRISTIAN ROCK
All Around Me • Be My Escape • Come on Back to Me • Hands and Feet • Million Pieces • Strong Tower • Tonight • We Are One Tonight.
00699824........................$14.95

72. ACOUSTIC '90s
All Apologies • Daughter • Disarm • Heaven Beside You • My Friends • Name • What I Got • The World I Know.
00699827........................$14.95

74. PAUL BALOCHE
Above All • All the Earth Will Sing Your Praises • Because of Your Love • My Reward • Offering • Open the Eyes of My Heart • Praise Adonai • Rise up and Praise Him.
00699831........................$14.95

75. TOM PETTY
American Girl • I Won't Back Down • Into the Great Wide Open • Learning to Fly • Mary Jane's Last Dance • Refugee • Runnin' Down a Dream • You Don't Know How It Feels.
00699882........................$16.99

76. COUNTRY HITS
Alcohol • Beer for My Horses • Honky Tonk Badonkadonk • It's Five O'Clock Somewhere • Lot of Leavin' Left to Do • Me and My Gang • Pickin' Wildflowers • Summertime.
00699884........................$14.95

78. NIRVANA
All Apologies • Come As You Are • Dumb • Heart Shaped Box • In Bloom • Lithium • Rape Me • Smells like Teen Spirit.
00700132........................$14.95

88. ACOUSTIC ANTHOLOGY
Don't Ask Me Why • Give a Little Bit • Jack and Diane • The Joker • Midnight Rider • Rocky Raccoon • Walk on the Wild Side • and more.
00700175........................$19.95

81. ROCK ANTHOLOGY
Barracuda • Can't Get Enough • Don't Fear the Reaper • Free Ride • Hurts So Good • I Need to Know • Rhiannon • Sultans of Swing • and more.
00700176........................$22.99

82. EASY ROCK SONGS
Bad Case of Loving You • Bang a Gong (Get It On) • I Can't Explain • I Love Rock 'N Roll • La Bamba • Mony, Mony • Should I Stay or Should I Go • Twist and Shout.
00700177........................$12.99

83. THREE CHORD SONGS
Bye Bye Love • Gloria • I Fought the Law • Love Me Do • Mellow Yellow • Stir It Up • Willie and the Hand Jive • You Don't Mess Around with Jim.
00700178........................$12.99

86. BOSTON
Don't Look Back • Long Time • More Than a Feeling • Party • Peace of Mind • Rock & Roll Band • Smokin' • We're Ready.
00700465 ....$16.99

96. THIRD DAY
Blackbird • Call My Name • Consuming Fire • My Hope Is You • Nothing Compares • Tunnel • You Are Mine • Your Love Oh Lord.
00700560........................$14.95

97. ROCK BAND
Are You Gonna Be My Girl • Black Hole Sun • Creep • Dani California • In Bloom • Learn to Fly • Say It Ain't So • When You Were Young.
00700703........................$14.99

98. ROCK BAND
Ballroom Blitz • Detroit Rock City • Don't Fear the Reaper • Highway Star • Mississippi Queen • Should I Stay or Should I Go • Suffragette City • Train Kept A-Rollin'.
00700704........................$14.95

Prices, contents, and availability subject to change without notice.

FOR MORE INFORMATION,
SEE YOUR LOCAL MUSIC DEALER,
OR WRITE TO:

HAL•LEONARD® CORPORATION
7777 W. BLUEMOUND RD. P.O. BOX 13819
MILWAUKEE, WISCONSIN 53213

For complete songlists, visit Hal Leonard online at www.halleonard.com

0509